"This book is a much-needed resource for the church in a time of advancing climate change and increasing natural disasters. Blaufuss beautifully grounds her work in theological reflection and practical, professional experience. She reminds those engaged in disaster response and recovery of the essential requirement to respect the wisdom of those directly impacted by such devastation. As a survivor of a major natural disaster myself, I highly recommend this book."

—SHARI PRESTEMON
Acting associate general minister, United Church of Christ

"Rev. Mary Schaller Blaufuss delves into creation theology, addressing pressing issues like climate change and the escalating frequency and intensity of natural disasters. She underscores the urgency and significance of incorporating the lived experiences of vulnerable and marginalized communities affected by disasters into creation theology. Drawing from her personal experiences, both local and global, Rev. Blaufuss emphasizes the importance of local partnerships and solidarity in seeking justice for those who often remain unheard. This work not only enhances our theological understanding but also offers practical avenues for engagement, making it an invaluable resource for those dedicated to fostering well-being and working for justice in the world."

—VY T. NGUYEN
Executive director, Week of Compassion,
The Christian Church (Disciples of Christ) in the United States and Canada

"Mary Schaller Blaufuss writes with the authority and authenticity of personal experience, and her insights ring true to our experience with disaster in Indonesia: earthquakes, volcanic eruptions, tsunamis, and cyclones, as well as deadly communal conflict. Disaster tests our theology like an earthquake tests the foundations of a building. This book is a guide for nurturing theology that helps rather than hinders."

—JOHN CAMPBELL-NELSON
Retired professor of pastoral theology, Artha Wacana Christian University, Timor, Indonesia

"Mary Schaller Blaufuss is uniquely qualified to write this book on disaster theology. Not only is she a careful scholar of Bible and theology, but she also has fifteen years of direct experience of accompanying victims of disaster and of planning effective, liberating, compassionate, and just responses to disaster. This book very helpfully addresses the questions regularly raised by people of faith: Why disaster? Who and where is God? How can we best respond?"

—J. CLINTON MCCANN JR.
Evangelical professor of biblical interpretation, Eden Theological Seminary, St. Louis, Missouri

"Far from traditional pious platitudes that can devolve into callous fatalism, Schaller Blaufuss draws on her vast experience of ministering among communities who have endured natural disasters around the globe. This book is a record and a guide for creating contextually engaged movements of solidarity in response to communities enduring disaster, and in witnessing to the hope of God's redemptive and reparative work active in these communities and movements."

—DEBORAH KRAUSE
President, Eden Theological Seminary

Joining God in the Thin Places

Joining God in the Thin Places

Theologies Active in Natural Disaster

MARY SCHALLER BLAUFUSS

CASCADE *Books* · Eugene, Oregon

JOINING GOD IN THE THIN PLACES
Theologies Active in Natural Disaster

Copyright © 2025 Mary Schaller Blaufuss. All rights reserved. Except for brief quotations in critical publications or reviews, no part of this book may be reproduced in any manner without prior written permission from the publisher. Write: Permissions, Wipf and Stock Publishers, 199 W. 8th Ave., Suite 3, Eugene, OR 97401.

Cascade Books
An Imprint of Wipf and Stock Publishers
199 W. 8th Ave., Suite 3
Eugene, OR 97401

www.wipfandstock.com

PAPERBACK ISBN: 979-8-3852-2777-8
HARDCOVER ISBN: 979-8-3852-2778-5
EBOOK ISBN: 979-8-3852-2779-2

Cataloguing-in-Publication data:

Names: Blaufuss, Mary Schaller, author.

Title: Joining God in the thin places : theologies active in natural disaster / Mary Schaller Blaufuss.

Description: Eugene, OR : Cascade Books, 2025 | Includes bibliographical references and index.

Identifiers: ISBN 979-8-3852-2777-8 (paperback) | ISBN 979-8-3852-2778-5 (hardcover) | ISBN 979-8-3852-2779-2 (ebook)

Subjects: LCSH: Disaster relief | Disasters—Religious aspects—Christianity | Church work with disaster victims

Classification: BT161 .B43 2025 (paperback) | BT161 .B43 (ebook)

VERSION NUMBER 041025

Scripture quotations are taken from the New Revised Standard Version Updated Edition. Copyright © 2021 National Council of Churches of Christ in the United States of America. Used by permission. All rights reserved worldwide.

Prayer: Natural Disaster. From *Book of Common Worship: 2018 Edition.* © 2018 Westminster John Knox Press. Used by permission.

Photos used by permission of Wider Church Ministries, United Church of Christ.

For Kurt
living the life of local and global ministry together

Contents

Acknowledgements | ix
Abbreviations | xi

Chapter 1
Introduction: Making Meaning for Sustainable Community | 1

Chapter 2
Doing Theology in the Thin Places: Theological Method | 21

Chapter 3
Rooting Natural Disasters in Creation Theology | 43

Chapter 4
God's Nature Shapes Creation and Its Flourishing | 63

Chapter 5
Accompaniment as Proximity and Connection | 82

Chapter 6
Solidarity Seeking Justice | 109

Chapter 7
Community Resilience | 121

Chapter 8
God's Sustaining Love | 141

Bibliography | 157
Location Index | 165
Named Disaster Events Index | 167

Scripture Index | 169
Author/People Index | 171
Subject and Organization Index | 173

Acknowledgements

THIS BOOK IS THE outcome of my continuing journey with people impacted by natural disasters as I bring a lens of theological reflection and encourage others to do the same.

I acknowledge first those who have experienced those natural disasters, your resilience, and all that your journeys have taught the rest of us. I do not take lightly the occasion to accompany you during these disruptions of life. And I give thanks for the inspiration of walking with you when hope and new possibilities emerge.

I give thanks for the hundreds of volunteers in groups and as individuals with whom I have worked through the years. You have immersed yourselves in disaster response, recovery, and rebuilding and changed lives along the way. Staff colleagues and friends in church and civil society organizations around the United States and the globe embody a commitment to long-term recovery that persists when public attention goes on to other things. I am grateful to be among you. I especially offer thanks to Susan Sanders and Florence Coppola with whom I journeyed on staff with the national United Church of Christ in volunteer, disaster, refugee, and sustainable development ministries. You model partnership and listening to local people.

This book is, in part, a spiritual autobiography that references pivotal moments personally and in public discourse that contribute to my perspectives. It is a continuation of the theological questions I first posed as a teenager to my pastor, Rev. Fred Wehrenberg, on "why cancer." His response that offered not packaged answers but

Acknowledgements

a foray into questions of free will for all parts of creation informs me to this day.

I thank my family beyond measure. My parents, Linda Schaller and E. John Schaller, provided opportunities that stimulated my love of learning and embrace of new experiences. My husband, Kurt, is a partner in life and in ministry. We have had so many adventures and more to come. My children, their spouses, and now my grandchildren are my delight. You have grown up during the events that are included in these pages. The world of frequent and intense natural disasters is where you live. I pray that your influence in these pages will empower and encourage your generations into the resilience of community that is beautiful and flourishing.

Abbreviations

Churches and Church Agencies

ACMNP	A Christian Ministry in the National Parks
CCDB	Christian Commission for Development in Bangladesh
CWS	Church World Service
IEUPR	*Iglesia Evangélica Unida de Puerto Rico* (Evangelical Church of Puerto Rico)
UCC	United Church of Christ
UCCP	United Church of Christ in the Philippines
WCC	World Council of Churches

Government, Civil Society, and Community Organizations

COAD	Community Organizations Active in Disaster
COP	Conference of the Parties, United Nations Framework Convention on Climate Change
DRR	Disaster Risk Reduction
FEMA	Federal Emergency Management Agency
IPCC	Intergovernmental Panel on Climate Change

Abbreviations

IRDR	Integrated Research on Disaster Risk
NVOAD	National Voluntary Organizations Active in Disaster
NRDC	Natural Resources Defense Council
SETCDC	Southeast Texas Community Development Corporation
UN	United Nations
UNDRR	United Nations Office of Disaster Risk Reduction
UNICEF	United Nations Children's Fund
UNISDR	United Nations International Strategy for Disaster Reduction
WHO	World Health Organization

Chapter 1

Introduction

Making Meaning for Sustainable Community

Personal Microcosm Moments and Collective Storytelling Make Meaning

Cancer

"It is cancer." I sat in the semi-dark room of the doctor's office with the glow of the computer screen lighting the hospital bed on which I had been sitting for the follow-up exam to my biopsy. Nurses had been doting on me and then leaving me to wait. The doctor had come into the room, left, and finally came back into the room again. She sat on her stool and rolled it across the room closer to me. With the news, I drew in a deep breath and my body tensed up. That was not what I expected to hear. In my mind, the extra mammograms and tests were just a life-scheduling nuisance, not a life-changing indicator. My mind raced and my heart jumped into my throat. My self-perception as "healthy" (a.k.a. whole and in control) crumbled. And the first words cascading out of my mouth: "What could I have done to prevent this?" In those moments of crisis, what is embedded in our worldview tumbles out.

We do not calculate or reflect. We act and react. The nurse moved instinctively to place her hand on my shoulder. The doctor leaned in. "Cancer happens." Silence in the room. I steadied myself and tried to hold back tears. Once the tears subsided, "Okay, what do we do now?"

Following surgery and treatment, I have been cancer free for almost ten years. I am privileged to have had access to medical care that enabled early detection and appropriate treatment. I am grateful for the people who love me and the communities that sustain me. Health, however, is not a destination, but a process. And my health is not separate from the health of those without access to health care or disconnected from communities that make them whole. The experience of that cancer disruption has woven itself through my being in ways that have contributed to my personal meaning-making and sense of life's purpose.

You might ask why I begin a book on Christian theologies amid natural disaster with a cancer story. I ask that too. But it is in such microcosm moments of our lives that meaning and purpose in the larger communities in which we journey take shape. This is one such framework for me.[1]

In that hospital room I tussled instantaneously with theological questions that also are part of the world's interaction with natural disasters. The intervening years of cancer recovery have reinforced my commitment to long-term resilience; a commitment shared collectively by communities impacted by disaster. Questions surface. Who is God as creator, redeemer, and sustainer? In other words: Why cancer? How to recover? What sustains the recovery and points to flourishing in the face of new threats?

Often those theological questions—who is God? Who am I and creation in relation to God and in relation to each other?—are not expressed in God language, but in our perceptions of ourselves and our role in that situation. The way we understand God impacts the way we respond in the world. Simultaneously, the way

---

1. I am grateful to have interacted with Jamie Aten, who also finds the shape of his work in disaster theology and recovery in the midst of his own cancer journey. Aten, *Walking Disaster*.

INTRODUCTION

we experience the world shapes the way we relate to God and one another in creation. God was present and acting in my microcosm moment of cancer diagnosis and treatment to create meaning and purpose. God, whose nature is relationship itself, moves through this world among people who experience natural disasters with similar meaning and purpose.

My experience of cancer with its diagnosis, treatment, and recovery interwove itself with my ongoing work in disaster recovery and sustainable development ministries. I had been accompanying people who experienced natural disasters before that microcosm moment and have continued since. The writing of this book extends over a couple of decades. During this time, I moved from direct interaction with recovery actions into administration in a setting of formal theological education. Part of this move was the hope to help shape the next generation of leaders for this work. It also provided time and space apart from immediate participation in recovery organizing to reflect on its learnings. This writing is a snapshot in time of experiences and reflections with a lens of theology on those experiences. It is part of my journey with natural disasters, theology, and long-term recovery, traversing the span of nearly two decades from 2005 to 2024. Situating ourselves in a theological journey is important for understanding the grace and the limitations of any story. The hope is that this rendering of particular stories and reflections creates a forum for you to engage multiple perspectives and interactions with natural disasters and theology as you join God in the thin places.

Tsunami and Earthquake

A global theological conversation on the nature of God in disaster emerged in 2004 and 2005.[2] I remember awaking on Christmas morning, December 25, 2004, in the US, to horrific scenes of the coasts of Sri Lanka and Indonesia as news began to filter around

2. This particular disaster event and conversation was a catalyzing moment for me. Subsequent chapters in this writing identify other disasters that also catalyzed global theological conversations and changes.

the world of the tsunami that had struck that part of the world and decimated lives. At first the news in the United States centered on European tourists whose family vacations were idyllic one moment and erupted in chaos the next. The suddenness and the randomness of the event caught everyone off guard and in disbelief. I remember my eyes glued to the screen, repeating over and over, I cannot believe this. Our family had been some of those tourists in a different but similar part of Sri Lanka a couple of years earlier. We were serving with the Common Global Ministries Board (Christian Church Disciples of Christ/United Church of Christ). I had been teaching mission theology and history at the ecumenical seminary in the south Indian city of Bangalore, the United Theological College. My life's academic passion has centered in South Asia, and I had recently fulfilled a dream of visiting Sri Lanka where the first missionaries from North America established themselves in 1820s. Those missionaries really wanted to be in India, but the British colonial rulers of the day and the British East India Company did not want any missionaries from the United States in India. Missionaries upset the status quo and got in the way of their trade relationships by bringing religion and the outside observers of another nation's citizens into the mix. In December 2004, I knew those settings flashing across the screen. Little by little, news commentators started to explore the stories of children who had chased receding water and the treasures exposed on the ocean floor laid bare by the tsunami. Those children were swallowed up when the wave came crashing back onto the land. It was heartbreaking beyond words. Local villagers made their living from fishing in the ocean. Their homes sat near that very ocean boundary to enable them to be close to their fishing vessels and because high land prices had pushed them off more habitable land. Their boats were gone, their lives lost and torn apart. The scope of the destruction was vast and disorienting. The unexpectedness of the calamity ripped apart not only physical lives, but any sense of security or balance in life. I did not know the names of the affected, but these felt like my people. I worshiped during that Sunday morning with those scenes running through my consciousness

Introduction

and my prayers, sitting near my close family, and feeling connected to that extended family in South Asia and Western Africa. The destruction made all the routine of the Christmas celebration that year seem incongruous. I pulled close to the theology of that Christmas moment, the incarnation. God's presence was among us in particular ways celebrated in the Emmanuel. Thus, began this part of my life's odyssey working with disaster recovery.

A week later I began serving on the national staff of the United Church of Christ as the executive for domestic volunteer ministries. This was a good fit for me because the role meant that I served on the same staff team as those of the denomination working most closely with partner churches and church-related relief organizations that were responding on the ground with families torn apart and then with the enormous situation of rebuilding. At that time, I was not in the position to make decisions on the nature of the recovery, but I listened carefully and learned. My experience in India had put me in contact with liberation theologians working close to marginalized people and reinforced the global church relationships that connect us no matter what our religious affiliation. I remained present. There emerged from this disaster event, and in the recovery, a global theological conversation among people of different religious traditions about who God is in the disaster event and in the recovery. It was a public conversation carried on in the newspapers and early social media of the day. It was not only a conversation about the nature of God, but also of the identity of people and of social structures. This was particularly important as extremes of social and economic inclusion/exclusion and of different religious and ethnic identities were so integral to the shape of the response, recovery, and rebuilding that did (or did not) take place.

Our theological starting point always matters, whether that starting point is formed by our family and traditions, by our claimed personal identity, by popular culture, or by reflection on our current experiences and context. In early 2005, theological responses to this tsunami seemed to fall into several main categories of emphasis. One, many concentrated on who to blame.

This response emerged across religious identities from village gods and goddesses to "world religions" with systematic and global cosmological and systematic theologies. Second, people who concentrated on classical theodicy framed questions as either/or. The divine is all-good and all-powerful. Or the divine is good but not all-powerful. Or the divine is all-powerful, but not always good. In a third category, others did not concentrate on the nature of God at all, leaving that to mystery beyond the knowing or the responsibility of humans. People in this camp concentrated on the individual and collective human response. They plumbed the nature of that human response, its motivation, implementation, outcome, and impact. That impact is the vision of what this response looks like when complete. Is this the well-being of all? Or is this human response governed by economic factors such as those described as "disaster capitalism"?

"Disaster capitalism" is coined to describe the phenomena that disasters can create a clean slate whereby new societies can be planted. The outcome is that what gets created usually benefits those in power. Naomi Klein in *The Shock Doctrine*, for example, explores how free market economics and privatization implements its policies in moments of cataclysmic events.[3] Or, is the impact envisioned as one religious or cultural group "winning" over the others as power dynamics are built or reinforced? This was an important component of the 2004 tsunami response because many of those most impacted by the tsunami were Muslim and many of the globally connected responses came from Christian bodies. Those Christian organizations were not of one mind or motivation. Some were there to use the situation to gain adherents to their own group or only to support coreligionists. Others lived out the missiology that places them in locations of greatest need with those who are most impacted no matter their religion, race, or ethnicity. This theology motivated global networks to bring resources to the community and preference the local community's lead to shape the response and recovery.

---

3. Klein, *Shock Doctrine*.

INTRODUCTION

Theologies in the Practice of Recovery

Eight months later in the United States, those conversations about the nature of God and the nature of disaster response reemerged as Hurricanes Katrina and Rita wreaked havoc on the United States Gulf Coast in an unexpected move of those hurricanes into the Gulf of Mexico. The fury of the hurricane's tidal wave removed human control from miles-deep swaths of land on the Gulf Coast of Mississippi, Arkansas, and Florida. Human-caused breaking of levees flooded New Orleans. Water filled the city and then it stayed. Issues of race and class glared in the multiple mistakes and prejudiced decisions on the part of human systems to respond or prepare and how they did that. Disaster landed on the forefront of television screens once again. And again we had a global conversation, this time not so self-consciously theological about the nature of God as it was about the role of government and social systems of inclusion, exclusion, and power. That part of the United States is often considered part of the Bible Belt and individuals use religious language freely. Survivors wove God-talk through their stories of the disaster event. By this time, my role with the domestic volunteer program of the United Church of Christ included working with individuals and groups of volunteers from all over the United States and some from other parts of the world who wanted to help with the recovery. In part, people wanted to make up for the gaps we witnessed in our government. In part, the media coverage had made the event part of our national consciousness. Like people in New Orleans and Mississippi, to this day, I speak of life before and life after Katrina as very different eras and realities.

I, like many who participate in disaster recovery, feel there is so much to do. Recovery can be so complicated interpersonally and socially there is little energy for stepping back to pay attention to God-talk that emerges from that disaster event and recovery. For almost fifteen years as part of the United Church of Christ national staff I worked alongside disaster recovery with volunteer groups and individuals. The last five of those years I led this ministry team working comprehensively with natural disasters, refugee asylum ministries, and global sustainable development. The ministry put me in contact with people around the world engaged in disaster preparation and long-term recovery. "Accompanying amazing people doing amazing things" became my personal mantra. The more I interact with survivors of disaster and with the systems and relationships of recovery, the more I am convinced of the need to pay attention to who God is in the disaster itself and in the recovery. I am encouraged to accompany survivors in reestablishing a framework of meaning and identity for themselves. And I believe we must impact the shape and systems of recovery for the sake of the long-term flourishing of communities.

Storytelling: Disaster Impacts Everyone

"Everyone has their hurricane story," began Gail Royster in my personal conversation with her in August 2022. Sitting in her home in North Houston, she recounted the journey of her and her husband, Rev. Bill Royster, in August 2005, the interim conference minister of the United Church of Christ's South Central Conference. These hurricane stories were about Hurricane Katrina in August 2005. The Roysters traveled south in late August 2005 from a visit to a church in northern Texas to the Conference office in Houston so they could be in place as a connecting point for displaced clergy and congregation members. Little did they know on that particular day what a vital role for the church this would be. The experience of that mass displacement over the next months and years emphasized the importance of an up-to-date church directory as disaster recovery tool to help make connections and check on people's well-being. During the next decade, the UCC Conference office, as a regional judicatory, helped organize, in cooperation with local and national resources, the opportunity for thousands of people from all over the country to accompany Gulf Coast people in their rebuilding and recovery. Eighteen years later, Gail remembered vividly that "everyone has their hurricane story" even while sitting amid a 2022 Texas drought with wildfire danger high, and hurricane season upon them again. A few days later, flash floods swept through that part of Houston. Persistent, frequent, and catastrophic disasters mean more and more that "everyone has their disaster story."

Storytelling: Human-Caused and Natural Disasters Intertwine

Natural disasters all have their human-caused components and disasters compound the difficulties of political catastrophes. The confluence of disaster and refugees and those forcibly displaced by disaster and by war is constant. In August 2021, for example, Haiti, the poorest country in the Western hemisphere, experienced a 7.2 magnitude earthquake. This happened in the wake of their presidential assassination the previous month and the political, economic, and social turmoil of that nation. Because I had been involved in the response and recovery actions after the 2010 Haiti earthquake, I could personally picture the impacted areas. I knew that schools in the northwest part of the country had painstakingly been rebuilt after the 2010 earthquake. People built them by carrying timber and materials through the mountain roads on human shoulders and donkey backs when trucks could no longer traverse the terrain. The rebuilt schools served as signs of hope for children to learn and to receive opportunities for a quality of life that did not hover on the edge of physical survival but flourished. And, now, here we were. Life was fragile and tenuous and not at all equal. People already struggling for survival were impacted most desperately. Their houses and structures could not withstand the quaking. People did not have access to health care or disaster response because of the isolation of where they were forced to live on the margins, inaccessible because of landslides that blocked roads and inaccessible because of the social and economic exclusion that kept them in poverty. The resources for recovery were not equal. Long-term recovery at the initiative and guidance of local decision-makers was hampered by government that has been undermined at every step. That government was in chaos with a presidential assassination even as the quake rocked the land; and

Tropical Storm Grace flooded the survivors. A history of international racism and structural slavery impacted long-term recovery.

At the same time, the twenty-plus year war waged by the United States in Afghanistan half a world away from Haiti came to a new stage in 2021. United States' troops were withdrawn from the country and the Taliban overtook city after city. Drought and its resulting famine among the people that had impacted the area since 1995 persisted. During the following year, 2022, a least three major earthquakes in January, June, and September shook Afghanistan. The quakes killed thousands and displaced more.

On a smaller scale, the state of Tennessee was struck by torrential rains and widespread flooding in which people were killed and missing and "homes washed off their foundations, cars strewn around the community." The Tennessee governor, Bill Lee, called it a "devastating picture of loss and heartache."[4] A week later, Hurricane Ida wreaked havoc in Louisiana, coming ashore as a category four hurricane exactly sixteen years to the day after Hurricane Katrina struck the United States Gulf Coast. Wildfires continued to burn out of control in California, destroying swaths of forest and human-populated areas.

Also in 2021, the Intergovernmental Panel on Climate Change (IPCC) published its global climate report, noting that the timeline has accelerated for a projected temperature rise to 1.5 degrees Celsius, "the limit scientists say is necessary for preventing the worst climate impacts."[5] By the 2023 IPCC report, "Human-induced global warming of 1.1 degrees Celsius has spurred changes to the Earth's climate that are unprecedented in human history."[6] The 2023 report summary observed with high confidence, "Widespread and rapid changes in the atmosphere, ocean, cryosphere and biosphere have occurred. Human-caused climate change is already affecting many weather and climate extremes in every region across the globe. This has led to widespread adverse impacts and related losses and damage to nature and people. Vulnerable

---

4. Lemos et al., "Tennessee Flooding."
5. Levin et al., "5 Big Findings," para. 4.
6. Boehm and Schumer, "10 Big Findings," para. 5.

INTRODUCTION

communities who have historically contributed the least to current climate change are disproportionately affected."[7] The world is currently on course to reach 1.5 degrees Celsius of warming within the next two decades. "Under a high-emissions scenario, the IPCC finds the world may warm by 4.4 degrees Celsius by 2100-with catastrophic results."[8]

All of this took place amid a global coronavirus pandemic of which the multiple waves and variants gained strength and disrupted communities. By the end of this writing, the coronavirus had become endemic. Other global disruptions, many prompted by or made more intense by accelerating climate change, erupted. The war of Russia versus Ukraine beginning in 2022 highlighted not only the horrors of a land offensive and sparked massive movement of people as refugees out of Ukraine, but also reminded the world of the continue dangers of nuclear weapons poised to attack. The interdependence of the global economy and infrastructure was highlighted with focus on oil and gas from Russia and agriculture, especially wheat, from Ukraine. In June of 2023 floods in Ukraine impacted the direction of the war and caused concern about the nuclear reactors under water as well as under attack. Intense drought in many parts of the world accelerated with heat waves and shifting rain patterns. Drought in countries on the Horn of Africa in East Africa particularly impacted agriculture, along with shortages of imports affected by the war in Ukraine. Famine increased. In June through August of 2022, Pakistan experienced flooding so extensive that two-thirds of the country and billions of people were impacted. Intense heat and accelerating fires are all part of the climate change that has now reached a snowballing speed of change in the planetary conditions for human life. Canadian wildfires burned swaths of forest in 2023 two months earlier than wildfires had erupted in previous years. Air quality across the continent impeded sight and breathing. In the war in Gaza in 2024, Israel fought Hamas by depriving the Palestinian

7. Intergovernmental Panel on Climate Change, *Climate Change 2023*, 5 (para. A2).

8. Boehm and Schumer, "10 Big Findings," para. 22.

people of water and food alongside bombings. By January 2025, the Israeli military had killed over 46,000 people in Gaza, mostly civilians, and displaced most of the 2.3 million inhabitants of Gaza.[9] Environmental disaster, widespread famine, and starvation is underway. Forced displacement, refugees, internally displaced people, and mass migration accompany each of these climate disasters and wars. Climate change catastrophes have become common parlance and are no longer exotic nor unexpected.

In this era of catastrophic climate change and natural disasters, which are intensifying and more frequent, we cannot avoid these catastrophes. When we do not turn away but pay attention to the complexities and to those impacted, we will gain a deeper understanding of who God is and how God acts. We do this by opening ourselves to seeing God's presence and action in unexpected places. We gain resilience to live more sustainably in this disruption-impacted world. And we not only have the motivation and the means, but also the vision, to accompany God in the very redemption and salvation of ourselves and of the world.

Defining Natural Disaster

Actions of Disaster Response, Recovery, and Rebuilding

Natural disasters are becoming more frequent and are intensifying exponentially. The pace of climate change and the inability of human and animal social structures to change rapidly enough for healthy adaptation is resulting in new and closer proximity of species sure to create more viruses and have viruses move among species more rapidly than in the past. Simultaneously, the world has experienced this year and in the past ten years more frequent and stronger hurricanes, typhoons, tornadoes, wildfires, earthquakes, and floods than ever before in recorded history. Sea levels are rising. Droughts are expanding in scope and length.

In many ways, a technical definition of disaster is superfluous to the theological project. Experiences do not fit into neatly

---

9. Farge and Al-Mughrabi, "Gaza Death Toll."

INTRODUCTION

prescribed definitions. Understandings of God and creation cross over among defined experiences. Disaster in its widest sense could be anything that disrupts stability and order. Categories themselves are porous. Every community disaster includes personal tragedy. Natural events are made more devastating because of human actions or inactions, whether that be climate change or the way that communities are marginalized and excluded.

The word "disaster" is used in public conversation to mean a wide variety of things. Disaster in popular use (and in the United States' response mechanisms) includes mass violence, which is definitely human-caused, and natural events with their human-caused components. In these there is a traumatic event that disrupts not only the lives of individuals but the lives of groups; it also impacts collective consciousness. Even for natural disasters in which some earth, wind, fire, or atmospheric change is the prime instigator of the disruption to the human community, there are always human-caused components. This is where, for example, the conversation about disaster and climate change fits. There are natural disasters that trigger technology-caused disasters in which human constructions are disrupted and cause danger and death through nuclear or chemical reactions as much as from the natural event (e.g., asbestos from falling houses, 9/11 chemicals from the destroyed Twin Towers of the World Trade Center in New York City in 2001, and Fukushima, Japan's nuclear plant disrupted by tsunami and earthquake in 2011.) Technology-caused catastrophes trigger natural disaster events, or at least the long-term disruption like a natural disaster event (e.g., explosions in the chemical dumpsites in Love Canal in upstate New York of the 1970s). Some natural disasters are quick and time-limited events at their most catastrophic. Long-term and long-time-coming disasters change the habitable earth forever (e.g., rising sea levels around the Pacific islands of Tuvalu or near Miami, Florida, or in Bangladesh). Casualty events with less economic destruction or death toll than numbers Federal Emergency Management Agency (FEMA) or emergency management systems define as disaster can also produce outcomes like natural disasters when they become symbolic and a catalyst for collective disorientation and collective consciousness changed. I am thinking here of the death of Michael Brown in Ferguson, Missouri, in 2014 that catapulted the Black Lives Matter movement into public consciousness with its exposure of racism and militarized policing in the United States with influences around the world.

This writing interacts with events and processes of natural elements (wind, water, fire, earth) that disrupt whole communities and cause widespread disruption and devastation, referring to them as "natural disasters."[10] It references disaster events identified with a date and disaster processes that unfold over time. No term can define all, but for purposes of this writing, components in the definition of natural disaster include: (1) disruption as dire as death; (2) large numbers of people and whole communities impacted; (3) earth component involved, terrestrial, atmospheric, fire, water; (4) symbolic consequences can be drawn that shape meaning and purpose. Changes in the community result. It corresponds to the definition of disaster by the United Nations International Strategy for Disaster Reduction (UNISDR) as "a serious disruption of a community or a society involving widespread human, material, economic or environmental losses and impacts, which exceeds the ability of the affected community or society to cope using its own resources."[11] The Integrated Research on Disaster Risk (IRDR) categorizes natural disasters into types based on their sphere of impact: geophysical (earthquake, volcanic activity), hydrological (flood, landslide, volcanic activity), meteorological (convection storm, extratropical storm, extreme temperature, fog, tropical cyclone), climatological (drought, glacial lake outburst, wildfire), biological (disease, insect infestation), and extraterrestrial (space

---

10. Other names for this phenomena and impact include weather and climate disasters. The National Centers for Environmental Information, part of the National Oceanic and Atmospheric Administration of the United States federal government, tracks data on weather and climate disasters. https://www.ncei.noaa.gov/. Environmental or ecological disaster terminology usually connotes a catastrophic event in the environment due to human activity. Diamond, *Collapse*.

11. UNISDR, "Terminology," 2.

Introduction

weather). This writing references events and their impact in the first four of these categories.[12]

Defining "disaster" is important for the present conversation because systems of preparation, mitigation, response, and recovery exist specific to these climate disruptions. "Disaster" presents a framework for expressing authenticity, authority, and accountability by giving direction for action. In the United States, for example, a whole system of public-private partnerships is in place for disaster response and recovery. Private insurance companies create a pathway to recovery for those with access to that insurance. Because the insurance industry's business plan is based on assigning responsibility for a disaster event in order to assign who pays the claim, the term "act of god" has emerged in formal insurance parlance to connote that no one could have been responsible but God. I believe this is telling for how theology, often unexamined and therefore misused, is part of everyday language. Use of unexamined theology shapes communities' understandings of God whether we intend it or not. Faith communities and faith-based organizations join other voluntary organizations active in disaster coordination of response, rebuilding communities, and equipping resilient communities for the long term. State and community organizations active in disaster identify unmet needs of local populations. Government organizations at local, state, and federal levels have mechanisms for first responders and directing collective resources for the response and rebuilding. Each of these mechanisms has its own sphere of responsibility.

When any of them are not functioning for the sake of the common good, the other parts of the system must adapt, or people and communities fall through the cracks—sometimes literal cracks. For example, for people in the United States and in other parts of the world without access to insurance or other collective safety nets, natural disasters or crop failures can be catastrophic. Amid the COVID-19 pandemic, people in the United States experienced catastrophic rates of illness and death because of the limitations and public discrediting of public health organizations and

12. Integrated Research on Disaster Risk, *Peril Classification*.

strategies. The global and local economic systems were unable to adapt at a pace fast enough (even with switch to technologies that made social distancing possible for some) to put into place safety measures for masses that enabled protection and well-being with equity at enough scale to stop the spread and subsequent mutations of the virus.

Natural Disasters as the Norm

As natural disasters become more frequent and more intense, they become more the norm than the exception for existence on planet Earth. Response organizations now treat natural disasters as the norm rather than the exception to life in a global community. The science arm of the United States Department of the Interior links natural disasters with climate change:

> With increasing global surface temperatures, the possibility of more droughts and increased intensity of storms will likely occur. As more water vapor is evaporated into the atmosphere it becomes fuel for more powerful storms to develop. More heat in the atmosphere and warmer ocean surface temperatures can lead to increased wind speeds in tropical storms. Rising sea levels expose higher locations not usually subjected to the power of the sea and to the erosive forces of waves and currents.[13]

Climate change accelerated by human actions or inactions has reached a tipping point where the earth's habitability and eventually sustainability is in question. Bill McKibben in a *Rolling Stone* magazine article of 2012 called this "global warming's terrifying new math."[14] Catherine Keller, writing on theology of apocalypse in the biblical book of Revelation, references the 2021 Climate Change Report of the Intergovernmental Panel on Climate Change (IPCC) that the world has moved from the need for mitigation to the need for adaptation. The point has now been reached where

---

13. United States Geological Survey, "How Can Climate."
14. McKibben, "Global Warming's."

stopping carbon dioxide emissions can stop the pace of climate change. She reflects, "Climate science has during this period shifted emphasis from mitigation to adaptation—a polite way of saying that the Holocene Earth, the world as we have known it for 10,000 years of so-called 'civilization' can no longer be saved."[15]

Climate change accelerates and intensifies the movements of earth change at work through the eons, so that human populations, as well as plant and animal populations, cannot adapt quickly enough for the survival of our most vulnerable of populations. Elizabeth Kolbert, writer of the *New York Times* best-selling book *The Sixth Extinction*, contends that cultures die because change comes too fast for them to adapt. She quotes Harvey Weiss at a Yale Institute for Biospheric Studies lecture in December 2004, "What Happened in the Holocene." Weiss observes, "You can argue that man [sic] through culture creates stability, or you can argue just as plausibly, that stability is for culture an essential precondition."[16] Kolbert and Weiss point to the idea of *anthropocene* as coined by the Dutch chemist Paul Crutzen.[17] Crutzen argues that human activity shapes natural systems so profoundly that earth's history has entered a new epoch.[18]

Nations are at risk of their land completely being eliminated by rising water levels. Bangladesh in southern Asia and Tuvalu in the South Pacific are two examples. The water and atmospheric events of hurricanes and tornadoes are influencing coastlines around the world and influencing the habitability of inland landscapes. Terrestrial changes by earthquakes, fires, and volcanoes are reshaping the earth's surface (Ring of Fire) to which human populations, societies, and cultures cannot adapt fast enough for survival of individuals, groups, or cultures. Kolbert observes that "dangerous anthropogenic interference" has now been achieved. "Hundreds of millions or billions of people currently live in cities that would be devastated by a sea level rise of twelve feet. That

15. Keller, *Facing Apocalypse*, 42.
16. Kolbert, *Sixth Extinction*, 119.
17. Kolbert, *Sixth Extinction*, 183.
18. Environment and Society, "Paul Crutzen."

process may take centuries to fully play out, but there's no going back."[19]

Theologies for Sustainable Community

Theological reflections that emerge in this book are an attempt at "expansive theology," a multistranded, intersectional, and dialogical journey. In other words, what follows in these pages are attempts to step back and listen to people's multiple experiences in disaster and recovery and to put them in conversation with each other. My constructive attempt then is to engage in dialogue with various subject fields. Theology is always emerging out of a matrix of experiences and articulations with multiple fields of reality. I appreciate the reinforcement of Catherine Keller's perspective in her writing on process theology and the apocalypse on the intersection of science and spirituality. "The theological spectrum on the left presumes, particularly in process and ecological forms, a long-term dialogue with the natural sciences."[20] My dialogue with quantum physics became important in my emerging articulation of the nature of God's creation as continuing creation. A dialogue with global, national, and local emergency management systems is the context of articulating cooperation and of visioning the role and purpose of accompaniment in recovery. I interact with social scientists, city planners, and economic theorists to shape my articulation of the nature of God's long-term steadfast love as community resilience. I am not an expert in any of those fields. But some of you are experts in those fields. I hope that this writing is an invitation for a public conversation about who God is and about who we are in relation to God and to one another and all of creation, for the sake of joining God in the redemption of the world.

---

19. Kolbert, *Sixth Extinction*, 193.
20. Keller, *Facing Apocalypse*, 43–44.

INTRODUCTION
You Are a Theologian

Disaster events and recovery give us an opening into that exploration of God and creation. In many ways, I believe that those who have experienced disaster and recovery are the most (or at least very good) authentic theologians because disruption and chaos and liminality are the very definition of having experienced disaster. Disaster experience is literally liminal: literally having life's boundaries rearranged. Disaster survivors and recovery community are not the only theologians, of course, but perhaps these experiences give a window into articulations and explorations of who God is for the rest of us and for the broader Christian community. As climate change strategies change, politically, scientifically, technologically, we also need more robust theologies to interact and guide that change so it becomes life-giving for all. We need each other, in the theologies already articulated, to enable us to survive, recover, and build resilience when experiencing disaster ourselves. And, in the new and more expansive theologies we express, equip others and future generations to adapt and mitigate climate change to lessen the impact of natural disasters. Practicing such ways of speaking of and relating to God and one another is a resource and gift that the Christian community can bring into long-term recovery. This gift accompanies people and helps shape societies and communities that are resilient and equitable, adaptable, dynamic, loving, and beautiful.

Liturgical Offering "Compassion That Makes Us One"

We learn and express theology through the songs we sing.

> Music: Dakota Hymn, Joseph R. Renville, 1842
> *Wakantanka Taku Nitawa* (Many and Great, O God, Are Your Works)
> Lyrics: Mary Schaller Blaufuss, 2021

> Earth plates will shift; the atmosphere whirls
> Fear, loss and awe abound.
> Seas surge to land; Volcanoes explode
> Things we have made, just tumble and fall.
> Who can God be? And who are we?
> Meaning? What can emerge?

> Some say, the end; or God is displeased
> Blame one another soon
> Cause and effect. Intense, getting worse.
> Yet, God's beyond and God is within
> Both are made real in margins of dread
> Multiplied grace makes new

> Jump in the fray, to act for the good
> Together, not just alone
> Hope beyond blame, revenge or control
> Glimpses of bounty, earth to be whole
> Sharing the pain. God won't go away.
> Compassion that makes us one

Chapter 2

Doing Theology in the Thin Places
Theological Method

Collective Storytelling Makes Meaning

Storytelling: Lisbon, Portugal, 1755—Triple Disaster and the Enlightenment

EARTHQUAKE. TSUNAMI. FIRE. THE events of November 1, 1755, changed Lisbon, Portugal, and the thinking of the Enlightenment forever. Blue skies and warm sun enveloped Christian worshipers in anticipation as they gathered in the Great Cathedral in middle Lisbon and in churches throughout the city. This All Saints' Day was a religious festival they looked forward to all year. Homes were decorated. Candles lit. And then, at 9:30 in the morning, the ground began to shake, more than a little sway. The walls of the cathedral shook and then began to break apart and collapse on the worshipers inside. Some in their festive clothes darted out of the church and fled to the docks of the harbor to escape buildings that now fell all around them. Others fleeing their houses and businesses in this densely populated city joined them. For ten horrifying minutes the ground quaked. Huge fissures appeared on the earth. Lisbonites later learned that people throughout Portugal and North Africa felt the earthquake too. Those who climbed aboard boats in the harbor or stood on the docks looking up at the sky breathed a sigh of relief. The harbor seemed to have more shoreline than usual. Relief. But that relief lasted only until they looked up and saw a huge wall of water approaching them. The tsunami caused by the earthquake crashed into the harbor and devastated homes and businesses through the shoreline of the city for miles inland. The giant waves crashed over lives and property a second and a third time. People buried under rubble or who rushed out of their homes kept the candles lit inside. Shaken, those flames lit larger fires that spread until they engulfed whole portions of the city. Artists around Europe and for ensuing decades rendered drawings and woodcarvings to portray the dramatic events of the disaster named "the Great Lisbon earthquake."

"The Lisbon Earthquake, 1755" (1850 engraving)

The multipronged disaster changed the political and economic trajectory of Portugal from dominance to destruction. Eyewitness Rev. Charles Davy wrote in his diary in translation, "1755 . . . That was the year when Lisbon town saw the earth open up and gulp her down."[1]

---

1. Cited by Wesley, "Serious Thoughts," 11:4.

The disaster also disrupted people's beliefs and frameworks of thought and of meaning. Some Portuguese Christian writers took the occasion to argue that the sin of free thought coming from the British had been visited with God's judgment. John Wesley, writing from a safe distance away in London, on the other hand, reflected on the Lisbon earthquake as "What is nature itself, but the art of God, or God's method of acting in the material world?"[2] The tragic events of that day thwarted the full-scale optimism of the Enlightenment. Voltaire, in his play *Candide* and other writings, argued against the optimism of the Enlightenment's central tenets that "all is for the best in the best of all possible worlds." Other Enlightenment writers veered from metaphysical reflections to seeking scientific explanations. Immanuel Kant wrote extensively on the 1755 Lisbon experience, crediting this event as the birthplace of the field of seismology. People rebuilt their homes in Lisbon as earthquake resistant. People spoke and wrote and thought differently about themselves and their relation to God and to creation because of the Lisbon triple disaster. The disruption of this disaster displaced people, economies, and politics in ways that shook them out of their assumptions and opened to them new relationships with God and with one another.

Storytelling: South Asia and Southern Africa 2004— Tsunami and Globalization

Natural disasters as "an act of God," "Is God in control?," "Who is to blame?," or "It's just a mystery" are among faith responses to natural disaster in legal terminology and popular culture informed by theological traditions.

When the earthquake and tsunami of December 2004 (see chapter 1) struck, people all over the world and in a variety of faith traditions reflected publicly on the God-meanings of this event, of the loss of life and the disruption to society. It was not only a global disaster. It became a global theological conversation: a God-talk

---

2. Wesley, "Serious Thoughts," 11:4.

moment. People asked the question early and often, "Where was God?" In a public dialogue that took place in the media, high profile leaders of multiple religions articulated meanings of the tsunami and of suffering. People in local Hindu traditions, such as those in southern Kerala, interpreted the wave as the anger of the goddess. *Kodalamma* (the Sea Goddess or Mother) is worshiped as kind, loving, and caring. *Kodalamma* gives fisherfolk their livelihoods and identity. People interpreted the tsunami as *Kodalamma's* anger and fury when people broke her laws.[3]

Some Christian leaders echoed this vengeance chorus and tried to assign blame to whatever cultural issues with which they were personally unhappy. Responses included God's punishment of the victims for past wrongdoing or warning to all humans of God's judgment. Catholic and Orthodox Christians joined in the public conversation by highlighting the mystery of God and how we cannot know God's intentions or actions. Christian Orthodox theologian David Bentley Hart landed theologically on the inability to explain the unexplainable suffering people endure, but gave permission to hate the catastrophe.[4] Protestant and Anglicans tended to avoid the question of who is responsible altogether and focused on seeing God amidst the response and recovery. Rev. Rowan Williams, Archbishop of Canterbury of the worldwide Anglican Church, wondered out loud, "Wouldn't we feel something of a chill at the prospect of a God who deliberately plans a program that involves a certain level of casualties?"[5] New York journalist Gary Stern observed that North American religious leaders tended to focus on raising money and awareness as the theological response to the catastrophe, not really addressing the nature of God in the disaster itself. God is inspiring donations. God is with the relief workers.[6]

Each of these responses is rooted in long traditions of God-talk and understanding. They address the nature of God. God is

3. Stanish, "Reflecting Theologically." Also see Tharakan, "Tsunami Story."
4. Stern, *Can God Intervene?*, 5, discussing Hart, *Doors of the Sea*, 101.
5. Stern, *Can God Intervene?*, 4, citing Williams, "God's Existence."
6. Stern, *Can God Intervene?*, 4.

all in control and we know why. God is all in control and we don't know why. God controls parts of what happens but not all. The nature of God shapes the kind of relationship possible of creation with Creator and of creatures with one another. It shapes the way natural disasters are experienced, the recovery, and the preparation made for the next disaster.

My own faith community tradition fell more on the side of God with the relief workers. God suffers with those who suffer, and the proactivity of God is present in the action of the relief workers. However, by leaving the theological reflection there, I believe we missed a chance to embrace the religious resources of our experience and tradition to explore and name who God is in the disaster as well as in the recovery. I do not believe it is enough to just say God is unexplainable. God is mystery, I believe, is different than God is not explainable. God is mystery, instead, implies that God is beyond explanation. It opens the way for multiple explanations. God's mystery gives meaning and purpose beyond what people can understand and connects creation to a divine that is bigger than us. To limit the observation, however, to God is unexplainable and remove us from the theological discourse is to turn over the meaning-making enterprise to those whose go-to response is to blame the victim.

Liturgical Offering "Prayer During 2020 Bushfires"

> All things look to you, O Lord,
> to give them their food in due season;
> Look in mercy on your people and hear our prayer
> for those whose lives and possessions are threatened by fire.
> Give protection and wisdom to fire fighters
> and other emergency service personnel.
> Encourage our generosity for those who suffer loss.
> In your mercy restore your creation and heal our land.
> So guide and bless your people,
> that we may enjoy the fruits of the earth,

and give you thanks with grateful hearts,
through our Lord Jesus Christ. Amen.[7]

Rapid Climate Change: Globe in the Twenty-First Century

The onset of rapid climate change is causing disasters that are more frequent, more intense, and longer in duration than previous disaster events.[8] Just in the United States, many examples exist. Superstorm Sandy (2012) in the United States was the costliest for recovery to date at $70 billion.[9] In 2017, Hurricanes Irene and Maria followed closely on the heels of Hurricane Harvey. People of the island of Puerto Rico, for example, had not even caught their breath from Hurricane Irene before facing the torrents of Hurricane Maria, which was even more destructive. Weather patterns creating oceanic disturbances named El Niño and La Niña create frequent disasters for the United States Gulf Coast from Florida to Texas.

These weather patterns are caused by rapid climate change. Change is happening so quickly that communities cannot adapt in enough time to avoid widespread destruction and disruption to societies. Eric Klinenberg reflects on social infrastructure as well as physical infrastructure needed to mitigate the impacts of natural disasters. Among other storms, he references Superstorm Sandy of 2012 and notes the continuing impact of sea level rise in Florida's Miami Dade County.[10] Miami Dade County of Florida's Sea Level Rise Strategy Project projects that by 2040 sea levels will be ten to seventeen inches higher than 2000 levels.[11] Planning for that impact on people, the natural environment, buildings, and

---

7. Anglican Diocese of Melbourne, "Prayer During 2020 Wildfires," Facebook, January 20, 2020.

8. Shukman, "Climate Change."

9. Rafferty, "Superstorm Sandy."

10. Klinenberg, *Palaces for the People*, 187, 190–94.

11. Southeast Florida Regional Climate Change Compact's Sea Level Rise Ad Hoc Work Group, "Unified Sea Level," 9.

infrastructure systems are underway. In his preaching and writing and advocacy on climate change, United Church of Christ leader Rev. Jim Antal is among a growing number who cite climate change as a primary cause of disasters.[12] Whereas in 2005, that assertion was regarded as an assertive claim by climate change activists, by 2025 it is a normative assumption in public discourse. The 2021 United Nations Intergovernmental Panel on Climate Change report backs up this discourse, showing how "the science of attribution linking extreme events to human-induced warming has become much more sophisticated, thanks to greater observational data, paleoclimate reconstructions, higher resolution models, enhanced ability to simulate recent warming and new analytical techniques."[13] David Waskow and Rhys Gerholdt of the World Resources Institute observe in the IPCC report that "human-induced warming has very likely been the main driver of glacial retreat since the 1990s, the reduction of Arctic sea ice since the 1970s, the decline in spring snow cover in the Northern Hemisphere since 1950, and global sea level rise since at least 1970."[14] Climate change that has caused drought conditions in the western part of the United States has brought with it concurrent wildfires that now happen on a large scale with regularity. The US has now begun thinking of the annual wildfire seasons along with annual hurricane seasons.

The June 2019–March 2020 bushfire season in Australia was known colloquially as "the Black Summer." The Center for Disaster Philanthropy estimates that forty-six million acres (seventy-two thousand square miles) burned, roughly the same area as the entire country of Syria. People lost their lives. Buildings and agricultural areas and livestock were lost. Several endangered species of animals were impacted, including the deaths of more than a third of the koala population. A loss of habitat will impact the species' recovery.[15] Black smoke circled the globe for more than three months. David Wallace-Wells reflects the change in approach to

12. Antal, *Climate Church*.
13. Levin, "5 Big Findings," para. 19.
14. Levin, "5 Big Findings," para. 20.
15. Wallace-Wells, "2019–2020 Australian Bushfires."

disaster for these long-duration events. He wrote in December 2019 about those fires and floods in Australia and the United States as semipermanent and normal:

> Today, there are categories of natural disasters, like droughts, we understand can last for months, or even years, and though they should demand our attention, rarely do.... But regarding the fires themselves—which can travel 60 miles per hour or more, creating their own weather systems that project lightning strikes miles away from the blaze, causing more fire—not as a sudden catastrophe but a semipermanent condition strikes me as another level of normalization entirely. And yet here we are.[16]

Wildfires in the western United States have continued to engulf communities. As of August 26, 2021, the situation report of the National Interagency Fire Center (NIFC) listed a total of 41,768 wildfires across the United States that had burned more than 4.8 million acres. More than 2.4 million of those acres were burned in eighty-eight large fires and complexes in thirteen states.[17] In August 2023 wildfires engulfed the island of Maui in Hawaii burning historic landmarks and causing over 115 deaths.[18] These disasters that happen with such regularity and intensity require a different kind of collective meaning-making than intermittent disruptions, even of large scale. They embody the reality that such long-term disruption could be considered "normal."

Theology in Context

Amidst such disasters, Christian theology has a role to play in meaning-making and purpose. It has a role in recognizing who God is and who we are in relation to God and one another. Christians bring resources of tradition, of experience, of connections,

---

16. Wallace-Wells, "Global Apathy," para. 8.
17. National Interagency Coordination Center, "Wildland Fire Summary."
18. Hawaii Department of Business, Economic Development and Tourism, "Maui Wildfire."

of revelation to this theological exploration. The exploration is in the thin places between God and creation caused and exacerbated by disasters.

Different Theologies—Different Outcomes

Mission theology from a strict Calvinism of the 1700s contended that if God wanted something done in the world, God would do it without human intervention. This theological approach still shows up in contemporary theologies of fate or of resignation. People embracing this theology may resign themselves to their fate with the faith statement that God is in charge. "That person is in a better place." "God must have a plan." The theology that undergirds these assertions wants to clarify the distinction between God and creation and affirm the sovereignty of God. A disaster caused by God's plan, or even by God's anger, may have been caused by the upset of the balance of divine-creaturely existence. Embracing this approach to theology is certainly a way of coping and making meaning of the experience. But it reinforces a chasm between God and the creation that creates a sense of fate and powerlessness among disaster-impacted people and affords no motivation for others to involve themselves.

Approaches emphasizing the strict separation of God and creation might also manifest in disregard for God or assume that a distant God puts everything into motion and then withdraws. These theologies assume that humans are completely responsible for things going wrong and for fixing them again. The strict division between God and creation separates one party or the other from accountability and response.

Other theologies rooted in separating people develop their own associated outcomes. Theologies based in an exclusivism assert that God belongs to them and does not love others. "God belongs to us" theologies motivate actions that focus on assisting people of the same religious group rather than those in most need. At their extreme, these theologies encourage responders to align assistance with persuasion for people to convert to their group. A "helping our own" approach may encourage impacted people to draw closer to those embracing such theology for greater access to recovery resources. Impacted people find ways to survive and thrive.

Theologies that assume the power of one group over another might manifest with those who have power "helping those more unfortunate than ourselves." This division might motivate assistance, but it does little toward drawing people closer to one another. Conversely, theologies of participation, especially those emerging in the nineteenth century over and against the strict former Calvinism, soften the gulf between God and creation. This approach recognizes that God works in the world through human hands and the actions of creation.

Theologies emphasizing God's love for all and calling people to come alongside others who suffer where they find God already present destroy barriers between people. Some disaster-impacted people might choose to become Christian from gratitude as they see Christians doing good and want to be part of a community in which actions and proclamation align. That outcome, however, is not the motivation to respond nor the expected outcome. A theology that moves from Christian exclusivism to God's love for the whole world in which Christians are invited to participate, motivates participants for social justice that shapes systems for equity among people and mitigates root causes that create disasters in the first place.

Theological Method: Authenticity, Authority, Accountability

All theology is contextual and experiential. Disaster as the context and content of theology, therefore, lends itself to a theological method that highlights authenticity, authority, and accountability. It participates in a liberating theology. Theology in disaster shapes Christian faith communities' participation in disaster response and recovery. Each trend in theology leads to a different shape of the response to the disaster. All continue to operate in people's examined or unexamined consciousness.

Acknowledging disaster as a context and content of theology moves away from a preset collection of phrases utilized at the time of disaster and recovery. It moves to a more holistic engagement in God-talk and God-walk. The act of doing theology, therefore, shapes the outcome of that recovery and emboldens emerging resilience. Intentionally reflecting on God in the midst of disaster and recovery creates a liberating theology and embodies a vision for flourishing, resilient communities.

Authenticity: Disaster Creates Thin Places and Margins

Disaster as disruption exaggerates the thin places in the lives of everyone impacted and creates disorder where once order seemed established. Disaster survivors, by definition, are marginalized. Disaster also intensifies the experiences of those who live every day at the margins of physical destruction. When earthquakes create a crevasse or crumble a building, survivors overlook the ledge of their previous physical surroundings. Disasters create psychological margins. When flood waters swallow belongings, survivors lose confidence in the safety of their surroundings. Trauma shapes people's responses. Anniversaries of a disaster often trigger emotional and physical fears as strong as the response to the original event. When hurricanes or typhoons sweep away swaths of buildings and trees, uncertainty embeds itself into people's lives. Every new crack of thunder or sweeping rainstorm makes survivors wonder if the destruction will overtake their lives again.

Theology takes place in those thin places. Theology in the thin places is experiential. Those thin places are where we, as creatures, experience a direct connection with God. The classical questions of Christian theology—Who is God? Who are we, as creation, in relation to God and to one another? These questions in thin places are no longer objective inquiry—about God; about humanity; about creation. Instead, they become relational exercises. Theology in thin places is an experience of God and an authentic experience of one another. Anthropologist Victor Turner might refer to this as "liminality."[19]

Many liberation theologians who experience God in the oppressions of their lives and experience the liberating actions of God through communities of the marginalized speak of "doing theology." People who speak of knowing God in nature testify to knowing God while away from human community immersed in the community of creation and open to the experience of the divine there. Natural disasters shake up, cover over, blow away, and open the stable, ordered, firm places in our world. Here, margins of the earth literally are rearranged, and disorder intensifies. Thin places are exposed, and God is fully present.

I contend that these thin-place experiences are among the authentic starting places for liberation theology. Experience of thin places in intentional ways adds to the theological roundtable to explore God's nature and creation's relationship to God. These are times in human history when increased and intensified climate change impacts humans and other life on planet Earth in significant ways. Disaster recovery and reconstruction will not be the project of a few but will be so commonplace that it is integral to who we are as earth-dwellers. Authentic and intersecting theological conversations from the perspective of this experience, action, and reflection enable more holistic participation in the journeys between chaos and order. Perhaps that movement already encompasses who we are, we just have not been intentional about putting God-talk to the God-walk we already travel.

Authority: Well-Being and Flourishing of All

Everyone is a theologian. We always are expressing our relationship with God and with each other and creation. Most often, that expression is not intentional. We go about our daily lives not questioning the cultures in which we exist and, through our participation, help shape. But in the thin places, that nonchalance changes.

---

19. Turner, *Ritual Process.*

Our lives must be intentional for survival and to accompany others struggling for survival. Everyday theologians might not speak, journal, post on social media, or publish our theology. But we are always teaching our experience of God to others. We embody and act out of whatever God-view we inhabit whether we are conscious of it or not. So, when we deliberately place ourselves alongside those in thin places of the world where we experience God, those theologies shape cultures, not just react to them. This marginalizing experience is the authority to understand who God is and what God does. We claim from the resources and experience of Christian faith with this authority that we actually join God in God's mission to make the world whole. We are integral to God's mission of well-being for all people and creation. We experience and help others experience God's mission of abundance and new life. These are bold claims—joining God in God's mission. Theology in thin places embraces God who is situated in that literal liminality and margins boldly creating, redeeming, and sustaining all of creation for the purpose of abundance and well-being.

Accountability: Mutuality Toward No More Marginalization

In a complex world, authenticity, authority, and accountability are intertwined. Authority is granted by the community based on perceptions of authenticity. Authenticity itself is defined through an accountability to others in service of God's mission of well-being and wholeness. Authority and accountability emerge when action and proclamation align. Through mutual accountability, we are responsible to one another for the well-being of all.

Natural disasters hurl impacted people into the cracks of life. Their lives are disrupted. They occupy liminal spaces. All disaster survivors stand in the margins—literally. Those already living in the margins are the most impacted by disasters and less likely to recover. Experience of disaster remains authoritative for a liberating theology because those at the margins live and act at the center of this theology. People who respond to or accompany others in recovery and rebuilding situate themselves to amplify the experiences of survivors and to carry their own interaction with those margins into the conversation and action.

The authenticity, authority, and accountability of liberating theologies is urgent in our time because climate change intensifies destruction. Climate change accelerates the processes of nature to create change on an enormous scale and in condensed time. Creatures and creation do not have time to adapt before the next huge change in the earth or sky. The delicate balance that keeps the interrelationship of parts of creation suitable for human habitation or for the survival of plant, animal, sky, or ocean life is disrupted on more massive scales. Disasters transpire with more frequency and intensity. The well-being of creation depends on actions to mitigate and slow the human-caused forces accelerating that climate change. Those actions join God's already at work to love and sustain the world.

The accountability created by this liberating theology is a relationship in which participants hold each other mutually accountable to actions at the service of a vision of the world in which margins are not gullies. Instead, they are connecting lines of interlinking and unimaginable beauty. Liminal spaces are no longer loci of pain and disruption. Liminal spaces, instead, are locations of creativity and new life. Lives are recovered and communities are rebuilt.

To be alive is to live in the constant negotiation of stability and instability. Living is a constant rebalancing of steadiness and change. Life includes form and structure as well as growth and adaptation. For me, the relationship between this form and adaptation is informed by Gayatri Spivak's work as a postcolonial literary critic. As a founding member of the "Subaltern Studies Collective," Spivak's focus is the subjectivity of those who are perceived as of inferior rank or life station because of the social group of which they are part. In her oft-referenced 1988 essay "Can the Subaltern Speak?"[20] she pushes back against defining people as subaltern or marginal as an essential category. If a group exercises agency, then

---

20. Spivak, *Critique of Postcolonial Reason*.

they are no longer voiceless, she argues. They are no longer "subaltern." That is the goal.

Likewise, accountability created in the liberating theology amidst disaster shifts power so that those in the margins and liminal spaces are no longer marginalized. That power shift is itself a rhythm of disorder and order; of disruption and stability; of chaos and pattern.

The goal of such theology in disaster is for well-being and recovery. It is for rebuilding of lives and communities. The goal is to create resilience and systemic change that leads to the continuous well-being of all, starting with the most excluded now. The goal of such theology is to live in dynamic interdependence with creation and therefore with God and each other, for the fullness of life and flourishing of all parts of creation. This liberating theology in the thin places that are created and exaggerated by disaster transforms those margins into webs of beauty and wholeness.

Natural Disasters in Biblical Theologies

Christian theologies utilize the Bible as a primary resource of faith stories and as a lens through which to experience and interact with God. Biblical narratives use natural elements and disasters for multiple purposes. God sometimes uses natural elements to complete God's intentions. At other places in the Bible, God uses natural elements for the purposes of judgment. Often, identification of a natural element or disaster event identifies a particular historical moment, rooting God in that context. Natural elements in the Bible also stand alone simply for people and other parts of creation to enjoy and to give glory to God.

Geologist Robert S. White identifies three primary ways biblical writers refer to disasters.[21] Specific natural disasters form a memorable event that is a point of reference. It connects you to that moment, even if you did not personally experience its immediate impact. In contemporary US culture, many remember where we

---

21. White, *Who Is to Blame?*, 97–98.

were when Martin Luther King Jr. was killed, or on the morning of September 11, 2001, or when we heard that the World Health Organization categorized COVID-19 as a global pandemic. White notices that a disaster might form the context of a biblical story. The context shapes the story, but the story's point is not to explain the disaster itself. White also notes that disasters are utilized by biblical writers as God's response to sin. The disaster is the consequence of human choices in the reality of the world God has created.

Terence Fretheim interacts more extensively with natural disasters in biblical theology. Terence Fretheim's groundbreaking theological work *The Suffering of God* has influenced generations of biblical scholars.[22] Fretheim's overarching thesis and contribution to the world is that God suffers with and that God is in authentic relationship with creation that includes being affected by that creation. God can change. Influenced by liberation and contextual theologies that start with people's experience and reflect on God from that lens, Fretheim's lens for biblical interpretation enabled my own interaction with biblical texts for a mutual and authentic relationship with God and with other people.

One of Terence Fretheim's later writings, published in 2010, deepened his theological method by specifically utilizing the lens of natural disasters.[23] I found this book as I was struggling through the writing wilderness of the piece you now are reading. I was at the point of simultaneously fearing that nothing had been previously written on this subject of theology amidst disaster from a progressive theological perspective and of knowing that this perspective had been formed through liberation theologians already accompanying people in disaster recovery. In November 2020, Dr. Fretheim passed away at the age of eighty-four. Testimonies to his work and influence from people such as Dr. Walter Brueggemann and Dr. John Bracke reinforced the importance of the lens of theology he opened to the resource of Old Testament, biblical, and theological studies in general.

22. Fretheim, *Suffering of God*.
23. Fretheim, *Creation Untamed*.

Like White, Fretheim also notes that biblical writers use natural disasters as historical markers. Disaster events are placed within the biblical narrative also to situate that story within real life and history. For example, the mountain or the kingdom is identifiable to those both inside and outside the Christian and Jewish traditions and therefore a point of contact for the stories' situation within the real world and at a particular time and place. This incarnational use of natural disasters in the biblical narrative establishes historicity and social location.

But Fretheim goes deeper. By interacting with specific stories, he shows how God uses parts of nature to render judgment on other parts of nature. Biblical stories affirm different instances in which the movement set in motion by God's instigative creating negatively impact other parts of creation. These judgments are intentional by God. God may intervene or catalyze creatures as agents, with small or dramatic action, to change the course in which the process of current creation is moving. In other places, one part of nature may exercise judgment on another part of nature in an unintentional way. God is willing to let creatures make their own decisions. In this, the possibility of beauty, wholeness, and newness emerges. But suffering and harm are also reality.

Storytelling: Tower of Siloam in Luke 13:1–9

Specific stories in Christian Scripture give us a window into those marginalized by disaster as do the theologians among us.

> At that very time there were some present who told Jesus about the Galileans whose blood Pilate had mingled with their sacrifices. He asked them, "Do you think that because these Galileans suffered in this way they were worse sinners than all other Galileans? No, I tell you, but unless you repent you will all perish as they did. Or those eighteen who were killed when the tower of Siloam fell on them—do you think that they were worse offenders than all the other people living in Jerusalem? No, I tell

you, but unless you repent you will all perish just as they did."

Then he told this parable: "A man had a fig tree planted in his vineyard, and he came looking for fruit on it and found none. So he said to the man working the vineyard, 'See here! For three years I have come looking for fruit on this fig tree, and still I find none. Cut it down! Why should it be wasting the soil?' He replied, 'Sir, let it alone for one more year, until I dig around it and put manure on it. If it bears fruit next year, well and good, but if not, you can cut it down.'"[24]

In a blame-the-victim society, Jesus reverses the responsibility to social systems that do not function to fulfill God's intention of abundance for all. We are called to be fertilizers of those systems of abundance.

Jesus uses specific events of his day and images of his listeners' culture to communicate the nature of repentance and grace. The events and images in this passage in Luke 13 would have evoked a visceral reaction from first-century listeners. They do the same for us. The political violence of Pilate resulting in the blood of Galileans and a natural disaster that destroys buildings and the people beneath them do not affect all individuals the same. The symbolic nature of these events becomes real in the experience of listeners of all time periods. Why do the innocent suffer? Why did this tragedy happen to these people? Why the seeming randomness of death and destruction? It is reminiscent of questions raised in Job, Ps 37, or Ps 73. It parallels the question raised in John 9:2: "Rabbi, who sinned, this man or his parents, that he was born blind?"

Jesus moves those "why questions" in Luke 13 from a focus on those individual victims to the society and systems of which they are part. "Unless you repent you will all perish just as they did," he tells the disciples (and us) (Luke 13:5). Fred Craddock notes that, in Jesus' world, repentance requires turning and change into a path of right relationship with God and with one another. "Life in the kingdom is not an elevated game of gaining favors and

---

24. Luke 13:1–9.

avoiding losses. Without repentance, all is lost anyway."[25] Corporate and individual repentance is the go-to response for Jesus because although the cause of the suffering is not the main point for God, the reality of those without power as the most vulnerable to political violence or natural disaster persists. People who live on the margins of society already struggle with multiple layers of hardship to which the crisis at hand is added. Those who already suffer also have less resources at hand or available to them to recover. The emphasis on societies and systems emerges from the spirit of the word *Ubuntu* from southern Africa, "I am because of who we are," or Paul's Greek nuance recorded in 1 Cor 12:26, "If one member suffers, all suffer together with it; if one member is honored, all rejoice together with it."

No, those eighteen who died from the collapse of the Tower of Siloam were no more "guilty." They were impacted by proximity to the tower—by happenstance. Or maybe the tower's infrastructure already was compromised in the first place. In that case, perhaps these were people already marginalized and could only gather in a place where the infrastructure was already unstable. Their blood had already been mixed with their sacrifices by Pilate. Social inequalities and injustice persist.

Jesus then switches from historian to storyteller in this Lukan passage to communicate the grace in this repentance. He refers to the fig tree and verbal exchange between master and gardener. Matthew and Mark record a version of this story as the "cursing of the fig tree" while Luke uses it to reinforce the grace in repentance. In all accounts, the fig tree is held accountable for not producing good fruit as is intended. In Luke, the master is ready to cut it down and start over until the gardener pleads for another chance. The request is not just one more year to let things ride, but one in which the gardener will fertilize and work with the soil so the tree will produce the abundance intended for itself and for the vineyard of which it is part. Craddock speaks of this as God's mercy still in serious conversation with God's judgment.[26] The master

---

25. Craddock, *Luke*, 169.
26. Craddock, *Luke*, 169.

agrees to another year, offering the fig tree with the gardener's accompaniment, another chance to be in right relationship as intended; to bear fruit.

The seeming randomness of natural disaster adds to the difficulty of experiencing the event and its aftermath. Life is going on as expected one moment and the next everything is thoroughly disrupted. Recovery therefore includes shaping a "new normal" physically, communally, and spiritually, assigning meaning to the experience. When that assigned meaning is to blame the victim, though, it not only causes more suffering for the group already affected, but also compromises the whole society. Jesus turns that go-to response of blaming the victim on its head, insisting instead on the responsibility of all in an attitude of repentance. Inherent in repentance is turning and change. That gardener is given the grace of yet another chance to be the one who fertilizes and cares for the tree, so it produces good fruit.

Jesus also is getting at this point with his story of the master, the fig tree, and the gardener. The gardener pleads with the master for another year's chance for this fig tree of no fruit. He does not just promise to stand on the sidelines and watch what happens, but to dig his hands in and fertilize the soil and change the very system in which the tree exists. This is all with the hope that fruit of that tree will blossom.

Systemic disaster recovery is about resilience as much as relief and recovery, and rebuilding is that fertilizing work in systems that created and respond to disaster, displaced people, and sustainable development. It is immediate care for the needs at hand; but it is also long-term and addresses root causes, digging our hands in, fertilizing the very soil in which we and our neighbors are planted with the intention to bloom.

Jesus may ask those around him the leading theological question to disclaim that those who suffer at the hands of political violence or of natural or human-caused disaster are the ones at fault. Instead, he calls all of us to repentance and to fertilizing work in the whole systems of which we are part.

Liberation Theology

This theology that emerges out of the experiences of people impacted by disaster is not only informed by the scientific worldview in which we understand reality in the twenty-first century, but by the experiences of those already excluded from the abundance that this multidimensional and interconnected world offers. Jon Sobrino, a liberation theologian writing out of the context of Latin America for decades, challenges all of us to prioritize the experiences of those the world's public discourse usually forgets.[27]

Liberation theology began to be named thus with the work of Gustavo Gutiérrez in the 1970s in the Latin American context of war and economic capitalism overload.[28] He wrote from the perspective of the church situated with and among the poor (as marginalized). The liberation theology of this era matched the international development discourse of the day in which economics were the primary framework of meaning. Unlike the development discourse of international bodies, liberation theology began with the voices of the poor and oppressed, listened, and drew conclusions and articulations from there. Paulo Friere's *Pedagogy of the Oppressed* operationalized the approach.[29] The hermeneutic circle expressed a method of theological articulation that started from social analysis and traced the connections between action and reflection. It was known as praxis, also drawing in the social sciences. God's nature in this liberation theology emerging from the Latin American context was rooted in the God of Exodus who heard the cries of the slaves in Egypt, equipped and inspired those among the people, and liberated them from the bonds of slavery.

Global theological conversations with the liberation theological method of starting from experience of the marginalized moved liberation theology also to incorporate theologies emerging from different identities. Starting with identities within the African continent context, the question of who God is not only

---

27. Sobrino, *Where Is God?*
28. Gutiérrez, *Theology of Liberation.*
29. Freire, *Pedagogy of the Oppressed.*

considered economic factors, but cultural ones as well. Feminist and Black theologies emerged from the personal identities of groups excluded from the power structures of their contexts with an essentialized single identity of a group or person as the experiential starting point. Womanist theologies have moved to incorporate the multiple identities that each person and group hold and are.

Theological conversations need to continue in this complex way, especially as we as humans observe more about who we are as individuals through a new age of science in which exploration moves us away from essentialized dichotomies of either-or. We live in a milieu where we relate to gender as a spectrum rather than as either male or female. We live in a world in which Heidegger's uncertainty principle has impacted physics and the way we understand the physical world in a way much different than the cause-and-effect mechanistic worldview of Newton. Today, the interlocking spiral of the DNA helix reflects and shapes our understanding of creation's reality. Those intersecting strands propel the shape of creation in multiple directions. The margins are multiple.

Liturgical Offering, Prayer "Natural Disaster"

(*Book of Common Worship*, 2018 edition)
God of earthquake, wind, and fire:
tame natural forces that defy control
or shock us by their fury.
Keep us from calling a disaster your justice;
and help us,
in good times or in calamity,
to trust your mercy, which never ends,
and your power,
which in Jesus Christ stilled storms,
raised the dead,
and put down demonic powers.
Amen.[30]

---

30. *Book of Common Worship*, 179.

Chapter 3

Rooting Natural Disasters in Creation Theology

**Personal Microcosm Moments Make Meaning:
The Gift of Randomness and Complex Order**

THE LAMP SAT ON the bedside table of my grandmother's home. The faded pink ruffles of its lampshade highlighted the blue-green hue of the bubble glass of the lampstand itself. The lamp fascinated me. As a child, we lived a few hours' drive from my grandmother's home. Visits on holidays elicited the comfort of time away from a hectic schedule. Home-cooked meals were the fare of the day, often with produce handpicked from the garden. As we arrived for a visit and the bedrooms were assigned to each of the kids, I always hoped to sleep in the "blue room." The walls were blue, as you can imagine. And on the bedside table was a lamp. We were not a family that freely told the stories of our past. But tracing the family tree of names, reciting who was related to whom, formed the content of many evenings around the table at Grandmother's home. That lamp centered stories that revealed some of the personalities connected to those names. You see, the lamp had survived a tornado.

As the German immigrants of our family had begun to homestead in southern Illinois, they prioritized clearing the land for farming. It was hard and slow work. The cyclone of 1890 that swept through the land cut a swath that would have taken my ancestors years to clear. It is part of my family's origin story of life on that land. But that storm also held terror. The family included four young sisters at the time. The parents saw the cyclone approaching and rushed to get everyone into the underground cellar for safety. Rolled eyes and a sly smile always accompany the story, even generations later. As the family ran to safety, the youngest sister, known to us as "Aunt Gusty" (Augusta), could not be found. Their mother located her just at the last minute and rushed her to safety in the cellar with the others just in time to avoid the damage of the cyclone. We knew Aunt Gusty for her fierce independence throughout life.

Home of Linda Horman Schaller, mother of author. Author's photo.

As the family emerged from the cellar, they encountered the destruction of their home. But as they picked their way through the debris, they found a glass lamp still intact. The trees they had been struggling to remove to clear fields for farming were gone. The family rebuilt their home. They farmed those fields. They passed that lamp down from generation to generation. Our family no longer lives on that homestead and those fields are farmed by others. A lamp seems relatively insignificant in and of itself. In my imagination as a young girl, it connected me with ancestors who had gone before me. In my interaction with natural disasters as an adult, the lamp symbolizes that connection to the resilience of independent Aunt Gusty and of a family with access to resources and community to recover and rebuild. But the randomness of that lamp's survival keeps returning to me as a symbol of the randomness and open-endedness of disasters.

A Rhythm of Randomness and Complexity

Reflection on God's role in disaster takes many forms. Many theologies emerge from assumptions of God's nature as all-powerful or all-good (*theodicy*). (See chapter 4 for more reflections on theodicy and the nature of God.) The concentration on God as all-good and all-powerful and the role of implied suffering leads to blame of the victims. God must have been angry and so caused or, at least, allowed, the disaster. Or, at the other extreme, the theology may not blame the victims, but relates to the disaster as so far removed from human control that no responsibility exists. The insurance industry in the United States, for example, literally uses the term "act of god" as a policy category to signify destruction that no person could have controlled. At either end of that continuum, the underlying assumption of natural disasters is of phenomena out of the ordinary, unexpected, and uncontrollable. These questions function to create a gulf between God and creation, including humans. When embraced to the extreme they function to remove responsibility from people to steward the earth to reduce disasters and they reduce motivation to respond and rebuild.

Instead, an authenticity of experience in disaster moves theology from reflection only on theodicy as the nature of God to emphasis on God's love and interdependent relationships and the resulting nature of creation itself. This reoriented creation theology takes seriously experience of accelerated climate change and the accompanying disasters that are more frequent, intense, and of longer duration than ever before. It resists climate change's continued acceleration and the accompanying destruction and disruption that are disasters. This creation theology informs disaster mitigation and response. It moves toward outcomes of resilience and wholeness. Creation theology can thus create the framework for reflection on God and creation amid disasters in ways that lean into a vision of beauty and wholeness for creation.

Natural Disaster Reorients Creation Theology: Questioning the Questions

To situate experiential disaster theology in creation theology requires a shift in the assumptions and outcomes of mechanistic theologies of creation. A journey through the biblical book of Job gives us a journey partner.

Book of Job

The book of Job is a walk through this very reorientation of the theology of creation and can serve as a framework for a different relationship of theology in natural disaster. It points to different approaches to mitigation, preparation, recovery, and rebuilding. It is a reorientation of our relationship with God and who God is. The book of Job is an open-ended, complex conversation between a yearning for order, answers, and structure with the chaotic, random experiences of creation that function differently.

Much of the book of Job chronicles Job and his friends reacting to their assumptions about how God orders the world, including creation itself. Job tussles with God and with his friends and family about who God is and what God does. At the heart of these conflicts is an assertion that claims the world is ordered and coherent. The early assumptions of Job and his friends about God's order correspond to accounts of creation in Gen 1 that focus on boundaries and form. Genesis 1 is all about differentiation and boundaries—the light from the darkness, sky from the land, land from the sea. The assumptions in this emphasis on form and order are based in cause and effect. Job and his friends all assume God created and ordered the world in a certain preconceived form. For them, deviation from that form means that Job or others who suffer went against the order of that creation. The friends argue that Job did something wrong, even if he did not know what constituted that wrong. Job argues that he is innocent and therefore should not suffer. He argues against God (this understanding of God) as unfair. He challenges creation as good and unquestionable. In Job 21, Job refutes point by point the assumption that God punishes the wicked. Job's soliloquy in Job 29–31 creates the argument "I am innocent."[1] In this reflection and questioning of God's creation and God's action, Job himself in chapter 23 is strengthened in his own resolve to live; a resilience. Yet, in both arguments rooted in the assumption of order, suffering is linked to God's retribution. The book of Job and Job's theological journey move to a different starting point in chapters 38–42, as we will explore later.

John 9

This Job tussle with an assumed worldview and understanding of God's nature is the same that underlies the question of the disciples in the New Testament book of John, chapter 9. While walking, Jesus and his disciples encounter a man blind from birth. The disciples' question is, "Rabbi, who sinned, this man or his parents, that he was born blind?" The question itself assumes that God created the world and everyone in it whole at the outset. Therefore, if suffering exists, it deviates from that wholeness. The chapter

---

1. McCann, "Job."

explores a cause-and-effect relationship that implies there is brokenness or sin that caused that disruption. There must be someone to blame for the man's blindness. It implies a mechanistic ordering of the world. Entire theologies of sin and of atonement are built around the assumptions of this question. They seek to find the cause, the one responsible, or the one to blame. It assumes that if someone suffers, they are not whole. It leads to a blame-the-victim response for challenges experienced. It leads to an apathy that just accepts injustice. Jesus' response in John 9, however, is to question the assumptions of the question itself. He immediately moves to action to restore the man's relationships in the community and to strengthen the relationship to Jesus himself.

Enlightenment Worldview

Likewise, a cause-and-effect theological starting point continued to underlie the Western Enlightenment beginning in the seventeenth century. Emerging scientific frameworks of the day assumed or pointed to particular forms of relationship among parts of the creation. In its emphasis on reason, the Enlightenment envisioned a mechanistic relationship among parts of creation. Enlightenment and modernity are built on a tight relationship between cause and effect. Isaac Newton's quantitative theory of gravity or the factories of the Industrial Revolution exemplify the direct causal effect thought to guide reality. One cause leads to one effect. The implication is that with enough information and objectivity about the cause then the effect can be predicted or changed. This understanding of the relationship between people and parts of creation has shaped our approaches to disaster into the twenty-first century.

Such a tight causal connection between cause and effect has shaped disaster mitigation by expanding capabilities to predict weather. Prediction has become big business and ways around which we order our daily lives through weather models and forecasts. Communities and city planning, insurance coverage, and politics addressing water and military endeavors are built around predictions of weather including terrestrial, atmospheric, or water events. Such prediction enables human communities to adapt to issue warnings and take cover, to make decisions on safe places to live and work. But it does not enable control of the wind, earth, fire, or water. Nor does it interact with the complexity of disaster implications.

Creation as Complex, Open-Ended, and Continuing

Book of Job

As the drama of the book of Job moves toward a climax, God finally breaks through the cause-and-effect assumptions of all the characters to turn Job's theological starting point on its head. God, having listened and stayed present with Job in his arguments of accusation and suffering, is moved and finally responds. Repeatedly throughout the book, the message of God to Job is that the world is not a tightly woven system. It does not run like a machine (Job 12:1–25). Instead, God makes known that creation is randomness, ambiguity, disorder, and unpredictability in its complex life.[2]

Divine speeches at the end of the book of Job are creation theology. Here, chaos is not only tolerated by God, but desired. The move toward open-ended and complex creation is a dramatic shift of those divine speeches in the book of Job. Barry Huff observes that whereas in Job 38, the desert is depicted as the end of human life, the divine speeches that follow open the world as bigger and more complex than Job could have imagined.[3] Huff explores the divine speeches' portrayal of wild animals and concludes that they are valued for their very wildness, not for their potential to be controlled. He shows how God has no desire to domesticate the wild goats in Job 39 but values them in their wildness. He notes how the Behemoth, a super creature beyond human control, is integral to creation (Job 40:15).[4]

2. Fretheim, *Creation Untamed*, 82.
3. Huff, "From Societal Scorn."
4. Huff, "From Societal Scorn."

Such embrace of chaos threads itself throughout Hebrew Scripture. The Leviathan is a playful pet of God in Ps 104. In Ps 8, God speaks to the sea, alluding to the ancient Near Eastern understanding of sea as unbounded energy. That sea is limited, but not eliminated. Chaos continues as part of God's creative intention. J. Clinton McCann, Psalms scholar, emphasizes that God has delimited chaotic forms for the purpose of life, but has not gotten rid of chaos.[5] Even in Gen 1, which is focused on order and boundary-making, the assumptions of creation are the starting point of chaos and complexity. Creation is not fashioned from absolutely nothing *ex nihilo* but is about the ordering and differentiating of that matter. Catherine Keller calls creation *ex profundis* (creation from the deep) in which the watery chaos has creative potentiality.[6]

The book of Job tells the story of Job discovering and coming to terms with a risky world as the way that creation is intended, because of that is the very nature of God. "Human suffering, even suffering such as Job's, may occur in a good, well-ordered, and reliable creation, because that world is not a risk-free world! God's directive to Job to 'gird up' his loins (Job 38:3; 40:7) calls him to prove his experience of suffering more deeply in terms of the complexity of God's design of the creation and his own place within it."[7] The divine speeches communicate God who works within creation for resilience of all creation, but not necessarily control.

Finally, in the book of Job, the response of God is divine speech coming out of a whirlwind as told in chapters 38–42. Here the divine speaker completely reorients the assumptions of creator and creation held by Job and the characters of the book of Job. Wrapped in this atmospheric disaster of a whirlwind, the divine speech response addresses the nature of God in creation as relational. Bill McKibben emphasizes this relational God and creation in *The Comforting Whirlwind: God, Job, and the Scale of Creation*.[8]

---

5. McCann, "Job."
6. Keller, *Facing Apocalypse*, 108n42.
7. Fretheim, *Creation Untamed*, 83.
8. McKibben, *Comforting Whirlwind*.

Relationship requires immersion in disorder, chaos, and risk not only order and stability. Terrance Fretheim concurs,

> The world that God has created is in process, and one effect of that reality is that it is not a risk-free place for human beings or animals. There is much about God's creation, beautiful and wonder-filled as it is, that is potentially dangerous for human life and health. God has purposefully created that way. And even though God has full knowledge of the world's harmful potential for its creatures, God did not provide danger-free zones for human beings, even for the righteous like Job. And that kind of risky world, for all the suffering that may result, is deemed necessary for it to be a good world.[9]

Multiple Religious Traditions

This immersion into chaos and disruption is present in many faith traditions. Those traditions signal the relationship between disaster and creation. For example, the Mayan civilizations of Central America and Tainos of the Caribbean identify Huracán, Hunraken, or Jurakan as a god of winds and destruction. The English word *hurricane* even emerges from this connection.[10] People in Hindu traditions in southern India worship Kadamma, the goddess of the sea as the one who creates, sustains, and destroys. Rabbi Myrna Matsa, working in disaster recovery in the US Gulf Coast in the early decades of the 2000s, begins a Jewish theology of disaster in creation, "According to our tradition the beginning was just that—only a beginning, as Creation was not yet complete. We human beings are intended to be God's partners and are responsible for serving as stewards of the earth's resources to harness its energies."[11]

---

9. Fretheim, *Creation Untamed*, 83.
10. Emanuel, *Divine Wind*, 18.
11. Matsa, "Jewish Theology," 1.

Quantum Worldview

The worldview of postmodernity and pluralism has also moved from immersion in the Enlightenment with its rational underpinnings reliant on mechanistic cause-and-effect relationships among God and creation and parts of creation with each other. Quantum science has influenced those assumptions. The contemporary worldview corresponding to scientific quantum theory subscribes to an interdependent relationship between chaos and creation. It recognizes both disorder and complex order. A quantum worldview can embrace creation in which wild animals, uncontrolled by humans, are integral to the creative intent of God. It questions mechanistic and causal principles as able to fully explain the interdependent interplay among order and form with the disruption of the chaotic energies such as embodied the Leviathan and Behemoth.

Changes in the natural world are accelerated by human activity. That activity and change is creating an unsustainable future because the systems of creation and human community cannot keep pace with this accelerated change. But change in the natural world is always happening. Change is not dependent on human control. In her work on climate change, Elizabeth Kolbert notes changes that happened beyond the scope of human interaction. "For the earth's flora, the last two million years have been particularly turbulent; in addition to the glacial cycles, there have also been dozens of abrupt climate shifts, like the Younger Dryas."[12] Kolbert notes that one can look at a map of North America circa 19000 BC and see ice sheets of the last glaciation having reached their maximum extent. The Laurentide ice sheet covered all of Canada as well as most of New England and the upper Midwest. Because so much water was tied up in the ice, sea levels were three hundred feet lower than they are now. The land mass that is now Florida appeared as a stubby protuberance, twice as wide as today.[13]

---

12. Kolbert, *Field Notes*, 83.
13. Kolbert, *Field Notes*, 84.

Rooting Natural Disasters in Creation Theology

Hebrew and Christian theologies point to creation that is disruptive, before and beyond the impact of human interaction. Earthquakes, volcanoes, floods, destructive weather patterns, cell mutations, and potentially deadly viruses were an integral part of the creation before human beings showed up. Fretheim points out that in the Genesis creation story of Gen 3:16–19, the pain of childbirth was increased. This indicates that there was pain before the *fall*, perhaps not as intense.[14] The biblical story of the flood experienced by Noah and family and countless others (Gen 6–8) also demonstrates that creation changes and destruction happens beyond the scope of human interaction. The tellers of the Genesis story of the flood do place the story in the context of sinful human community. And that is the emphasis given many interactions with this text in relation to disasters. People sin. God punishes. Full stop. But the story actually is more complex. People and societies already exist beyond the scope of this flood. The flood story parallels and emerged from other Babylonian stories of great floods in the region, such as the story of Gilgamesh. And the story's turning point (Gen 8:1) comes as God remembers Noah, his family, the animals. The attention in the text shifts to a focus on salvation rather than judgment. The promise of God for the continuation of creation is sealed with the sign of a bow in the sky.[15]

Complexity as Patterns of Connection

God is within time and beyond time. God is both/and. In the interplay between order and disruption, between chaos and stability, emerges the nature of God and the relationship of creation with God and each other. For there to be life, there is a constant interplay between chaos and order. The human body, for example, is constantly moving, and yet there is a discernible shape and form of what is a human body and not the body of something or someone else. In disruption, we always tend toward structure and stability.

---

14. Fretheim, *Creation Untamed*, 2.
15. Fretheim, *Creation Untamed*, 46.

In the material world, life, by definition, means movement and change. When those parts of creation stop moving and changing, then it is no longer life. Disruption and chaos then are also part and parcel of life by its very being.

At the same time, this complex and interdependent creation is not without pattern. Humans and all creation need stability and order to exist, to be defined and claim identity. Creation has structure. Scientist John Polkinghorne reminds us that in complex systems, physical processes must have dual character. They involve both energy and pattern. Polkinghorne observes, "The future behavior of a chaotic system is not totally haphazard. It displays a kind of orderly disorder. What will happen is not predictable, but it is confined within a large but restricted range of possibilities that technically is called a 'strange attractor.'"[16]

The pattern and order in this complex system can be imagined. Sometimes that disorder and reordering is incremental to the extreme like a river cutting through rock to form the Grand Canyon or a gorge in upstate New York. Or it can be sudden and catastrophic like an earthquake in Haiti or volcano in Hawaii.

---

16. Polkinghorne, "Kenotic Creation," 99.

Rooting Natural Disasters in Creation Theology

Watkins Glen State Park, New York. Photo by author.

In the infinite complexity that is creation, there is still order. Fractals are copies of an original into infinity. "Strange attractors" provide structure within chaos. "Period doubling" is a property of universality in which one property is the same for all systems.

In exploring the intersection of science and theology, Arthur Peacocke, scientist and theologian, reinforces this intersection of order and randomness. It is the combination of the two that makes possible an ordered universe capable of developing within itself new modes of existence.

> It has become increasingly apparent that it is chance operating within a law-like framework that is the basis of the inherent creativity of the natural order, its ability

> to generate new forms, patterns, and organizations of matter and energy. If all were governed by rigid law, a repetitive and uncreative order would prevail; if chance alone ruled, no forms, patterns or organizations would persist long enough for them to have any identity or real existence. It would be either a rigid repetitive machine or a primeval Hesiodic chaos.[17]

At the same time, observable and measurable characteristics that are predictable and universal, over the long term are not predictable. Turbulence and frequencies like water eddies and flow may have observable patterns, but their long-term behavior is inherently unpredictable. For example, the Grand Canyon with its majestic beauty is created through a process of destruction caused over time by water that is observable, but the outcome of what is created could be changed by any number of interdependent energies and actions.

Open-Ended Is "Good Not Perfect"

Such a multicausal way of experiencing the world helps illustrate the way God operates as creator and in the creation that emerges. What God creates is thoroughly connected to God's very nature. Creation is complex and connected. God's actions also make creation ongoing, open ended, and relational. The creation that emerges from that action and presence of God is the way it is (has its nature) because of the way God created it.

Terence Fretheim very helpfully summarizes God's nature in creation with the phrase "God created the world good, not perfect." Consider this phrase. It lifts the self-imposed pressure off creation and off us to twist ourselves into theological knots to explain or explain away parts of creation that do not fit our own perception of "perfection." Fretheim contends that *good* is an evaluative term. It corresponds to the divine intention that includes elements of beauty, purposefulness, praiseworthiness. *Good* implies developing toward the fullest possible potential. "This potential of

17. Peacocke, "Cost of New Life," 26.

becoming is built into the very structures of the world." *Perfect* in vernacular English usage usually refers to something without fault, defect, or inadequacy. To be what it is truly, something that is *perfect*, it has no need for improvement or development. Instead, as Fretheim points out from his study of Christian Scripture, creativity is inherent in creation. "God observes a decisive continuity between God's intention and the creational result."[18]

Creation as *perfect* would be limiting. It would imply that "It is what it is," "What you see is what you get." The theological imagination then is that if humans just understood the wholeness of creation, then we could control it. Open-ended creation, however, emphasizes the difference between God and humanity. God is God and creatures are creation. And it sets up the possibility for creation to be more beautiful than any part of creation or creature could imagine, reflecting glimmers of the glory of God.

Creation is, instead, *good*, and continuing. God created each part of creation whole, but not full. God's creation can still become. It can still move, live, and transform constantly. Creation continues to develop and becomes more and ever new. In examining the first two chapters of Genesis, Fretheim observes that "this spirit image of creation signals a dynamic rather than a static creative process, an open process rather than one that is tightly controlled."[19]

Arthur Peacocke observes that in the Hebrew conception of *living God* that God gives continuous existence to a process that has an inbuilt creativity. God builds that creativity into the ongoing process. In time, the result is existence. Peacocke uses the term *semper Creator* as his term for God. This means that creating is the very nature of God. Creation is not just an event in the past. It is not a finished product. Creation is dynamic today and into the future. Creation is energy, change, movement. God's creation is continuing creation.[20]

---

18. Fretheim, *Creation Untamed*, 13.
19. Fretheim, *Creation Untamed*, 21.
20. Peacocke, "Cost of New Life," 23.

Continuing Creation

This open-endedness of continuing creation is full of constant change. To live is to be constantly moving. God creates a dynamic world in which the future is open to many possibilities and in which creaturely activity is crucial for proper creational development.

Think of the flow of blood through the human body. When that movement stops, so does life itself. And in that movement, there is simultaneously both creation and disruption taking place. It can be the dramatic shift of tectonic plates that caused the Mississippi River to flow backwards and change course in 1812, creating a riverbed that flows today far from the bluffs in St. Louis; or the slow carving of water dripping that forms caves and molds landscapes (see chapter 2.) This constant change signals the type of creator God is. God creates this world that is constantly changing. Therefore, to live in this world means to live in that constant change. And sometimes when that change is dramatic, creatures are in the locations that get hurt.

That constant change means constant destruction as well as constant creation. God is giving creation the continuing capacity to be itself, to be what it was created to be, and also to develop into something more. God is creating in and through parts of creation already present. This continuing creation can be seen in Ps 104:30 in which the spirit working in and through existing creatures enables newness to emerge. "When you send forth your spirit, they are created; and you renew the face of the ground." Fretheim reflects, "The seeds of destruction are contained in the very nature of the situation, and God mediates those consequences."[21]

It is through constant change, disruption, and complex ordering that God creates within the very nature of the created. No linear cause and effect or blueprint leads to a particular effect or outcome. Instead, each part of creation has free will to be more than it was created to be. And in that more than state, there is also the opportunity to be less than (limited) or creative in manners that are not feeding the common good but are plotting toward

21. Fretheim, *Creation Untamed*, 22.

selfishness or destruction. Cancer cells are destructive because they are too creative or a destructive creation. The cells that multiply are the wrong cells for the common good of the body or multiply in ways disproportionate to what is needed for the journey of life of the body as a whole and therefore take it over, leading ultimately to the destruction of the body rather than its enlivening. God's creative activity requires disorder and open ends for the possibilities to become new and more than the current reality.

Job Recants and Changes

We return to the book of Job on the journey of expansive creation theology. In listening to God, Job recants (turns) in these assumptions and recognizes that God's presence and action in the world is what is different than he assumed (Job 42). The theological starting point changes to grace and trust rather than blame or cause and effect. The outcome from God for Job is education (he learns about God) and humility (God is God, and is fully present in creation, including its suffering) rather than humiliation or retribution. The impact is redemption by God who is God by being fully present and active in creation, in true relationship of love and trust, that includes suffering and responding and moving and continuing creation.

People Make Creation Into Disasters

Lest I have come across as too complacent in the catastrophe before us amid climate change, let me reiterate. Climate change is real. Disaster is devastating and its destruction evil. The argument here is that relating to disaster through a mechanistic cause-and-effect understanding of creation prevents human society from making the changes to mitigate and prevent that destruction.

Changes in creation are random, chaotic, and continuing. But the earth is changing at such a rapid pace that civilization and society cannot keep up. What human activities, sins, and limitations of creation do is to intensify and make the changes of creation more frequent and catastrophic, causing disruption and disaster for other parts of creation. Theologians from such disparate perspectives as the Christian process theology of Catherine Keller and the eco-advocacy of Bill McKibben communicate the dire state of this change that is too rapid. Harry O. Maier and Catherine Keller note that in the biblical book of Revelation, ecological disaster portrays the broken relations between humans and with God.[22] Human activity accelerates that change to the degree that it moves more quickly than human societies and cultures can adapt. That inability to adapt creates catastrophic and ongoing disasters. Bill McKibben, eco-activist, claims that "we are running Genesis backwards, de-creating."[23] He compares the breathtaking picture of "earth rising" as seen from the spaceship Apollo 8 orbit in 1968 to the picture of earth in 2010 with its profound climate change in such a short period. In a catalogue of anecdotes of dramatic climate change observations and agency reports, just from the years 2007 to 2009, McKibben vividly shows how climate change has forever altered our world with no going back. "The world hasn't ended, but the world as we know it has—even if we don't quite know it yet . . . it's a different place. A different planet. It needs a new name, *Eaarth*."[24]

A Turning Point for Relationship with God

The lens of the randomness of disaster experiences contributes to understanding and relating to God and one another by turning theology to the complexity of the created world and of creatures. Although creation and creatures need order to survive, the very nature of creation is interdependent complexity. Randomness and chaos are not disorder, but complex complexity.

The more we know of the layers of this complexity through scientific methods of astronomy, chaotic dynamics, and quantum

---

22. Keller, *Facing Apocalypse*, 46n46.
23. McKibben, *Eaarth*, 25.
24. McKibben, *Eaarth*, 2.

theories, the more this complexity shows. It is a complexity that is interdependent and not connected in a tight causal weave. Indeed, natural disasters and their catastrophic destruction demonstrate the danger of this randomness. It also is a complexity that carries the possibilities of beauty beyond imagination.

Coming to terms with the reality of randomness and the creativity of chaos opens our theology to interaction with the complexity and open-endedness of continuing creation. It changes our relationship with God and with one another in creation. Jim Antal, in reflecting on climate change and the role of the church, concludes,

> Yes—God still has a dream. As broken-hearted as God must be over what we have done to the gift of creation, God still has a dream. However much we rebel, however much we ignore God's instructions, however much we abuse God's gift of creation, we cannot diminish the power of God's dream. It is a dream anchored in love, not exploitation. It is a dream in which every living thing is a reflection of God, vibrantly alive with grateful, joyful hearts. In God's dream, everyone has enough and all are beneficiaries of God's abundance. God dreams that humans seek spiritual rather than material progress. God's dream envisions a just world at peace because gratitude has dissolved anxiety and generosity has eclipsed greed. God dreams of a time when love and mutual respect will bind humanity together, and the profound beauty of creation will be treasured.[25]

Accompanying Job on his journey of theological reorientation also changes our own relationship with God. God's continuing creation of open-endedness and complexity enables our relationship with God and creation in ways that are life giving. Opening ourselves to such possibilities situates us amid that creativity and complexity in ways that connect us to God's own creative activities. We then are empowered to work against injustices that cause greater impact of disasters on vulnerable people and to work to slow climate change and the accompanying catastrophic

---

25. Antal, *Climate Church*, 169.

destruction of disasters. We are reoriented to a relationship with God who is connectional, creative, and loving.

Chapter 4

God's Nature Shapes Creation and Its Flourishing

Personal Microcosm Moments Make Meaning: The Challenge of Randomness

ONE OF THE MOST difficult things about experiencing a natural disaster is the randomness of the effects of the disaster itself. Paying attention to that randomness gives us insight into the nature of creation and of God. I remember driving on Highway 90 along the Mississippi Gulf Coast in the fall of 2005, just months after Hurricane Katrina had destroyed lives and communities. I served as the point person in the United Church of Christ national ministries to work with local partners and organize opportunities for people throughout the country to accompany the cleanup and rebuilding. People on the Gulf Coast and those of us from outside struggled to know where to begin or how to make an impact. The destruction still felt dizzying. During that drive, I looked to one side of the highway where waters of the Gulf of Mexico stretched serene and blue to the horizon and beyond. A slight twist of my neck though revealed the other side of the highway lined with mangled branches of once stately oak trees. Random white and blue plastic bags hung in those branches waving in the sea breeze as if replacements for once splendid leaves. I saw concrete steps rising from housing foundations, now leading to nothing. The storm swept whole houses out to sea. Other homes though remained virtually untouched as the waters moved right past or through them. The disaster's eeriness and randomness loomed large on that stretch of highway.

Highway 90, Biloxi, Mississippi, October 2005.
Photo by author, credit Wider Church Ministries, United Church of Christ

Lower Ninth Ward, New Orleans, Louisiana, December 2006.
Photo by author, credit Wider Church Ministries, United Church of Christ.

I stayed hyperaware of the randomness inherent in disaster experience as I helped the church organize volunteers from outside other impacted areas to assist with response and rebuilding. Tornadoes create sporadic impact. I stood with people in Moore, Oklahoma, in 2008, for example, to mourn as swirling winds swept up every home on one side of the street. Homes on the other side of the street though remained untouched. Not *fair* or explainable.

Earthquakes create cracks and thin places where previously none existed. That randomness is real, with life-and-death consequences. Rick Santos, current president and CEO of Church World Service, survived the devastating Haiti earthquake of 2010. His story inspires. In 2010, Santos worked with another church organization, IMA World Health. He and others from Haiti and the United States gathered at a hotel in the capital city of Port-au-Prince to discuss strategy for eliminating neglected tropical diseases from country. As the earthquake struck unexpectedly, the building collapsed around the group. Beams from the ceiling and concrete from the walls of the building struck many, killing them instantly or trapping them before they succumbed to injuries. Santos himself remained buried under tons of rubble for three nights. Disaster responders did find and rescue him. The earthquake, though, was one of the worst disasters this century, killing an estimated 250,000 people and injuring hundreds of thousands more. Santos continues to organize disaster response around the world in his leadership of Church World Service. He carries the randomness of his experience of life and death.[1]

Humans need order and form to exist and to make meaning. Disaster experience exaggerates the reality of randomness inherent in all of creation. How do we reconcile that experience of disorder and disruption with the need for order? Where do we see God in this experience of randomness? God is right in the heart of it, experiencing that disruption along with creation. To acknowledge that randomness opens us to God's presence that embodies mutual accountability among all parts of that creation. God's presence provides the stability to make meaning and to move through the brokenness toward wholeness.

Classical Theodicy and Suffering

Many theologies of disaster focus on God and suffering. How could God let—or make—this happen? This question of classical theodicy attempts to make rational sense of evil and suffering rooted in assumptions of God's nature as all-knowing, all-powerful, and all-good. In classical theodicy and in much popular religiosity, God either cannot or will not prevent catastrophes. Such theologies even point to God as deliberately causing disasters to punish creatures. The theodicy question that assumes God is all-powerful and all-good depends on a tight causal weave between morals and power. It assumes a mechanistic view of creation. Classical theodicies assume that randomness and chaos are anomalies or deficits in creation itself. Tragedy, therefore, induces submissiveness. "It is God's will."

Philosophers and Christian theologians through many centuries shape this popular religiosity by identifying the dilemma

---

1. Santos, "What Led Me."

God's Nature Shapes Creation and Its Flourishing

created at this disjuncture of a tight causal weave between morals and power with attempts to explain it into a cohesive whole. The Greek philosopher Epicurus (341–270 BC) used rational logic to express the dilemma of God's nature.

> Either God does not want to eliminate evil, or he cannot; either he can but does not want to; or he cannot and does not want to; or he wants to and can. If he can and does not want, then he is evil, which must be against God's nature. If he does not want to and cannot, then he is evil and weak, and therefore he is not God. If he can and wants to, which can only be true of God, then where does evil come from and why does he not eliminate it.[2]

Irenaeus of Lyons in the second century (AD 130–202) influenced Eastern Christianity. For Irenaeus, evil exists to allow humans to develop as moral agents with free will. Suffering produces goodness.[3] Augustine of Hippo in North Africa (AD 354–430) influenced Western Christianity. For Augustine, God created the world without evil or suffering. The existence of such is punishment for original sin.

The Enlightenment and Protestant Reformation era beginning in the fifteenth century questioned these hierarchical understandings of God. In understandings of God as all-powerful or all-good, suffering is seen as limitation interpreted as a bad thing. God, in this view, created the world as all whole and all good. Sin broke that wholeness and caused suffering. Scientific breakthroughs of the Enlightenment era questioned hierarchical authority, even of God-understandings. German theologian (and mathematician) Gottfried Leibniz used the term in his 1710 book *Theodicee*. All tried to make sense of the reality of evil and suffering. Following the 1755 Lisbon earthquake, Voltaire's bitter reflection on God and lack of fairness ended rationalist optimism expressed by those such as Leibniz.[4] "If the only way we can excuse God is by confess-

---

2. Sobrino, *Where Is God?*, 141.
3. Hick, *Evil*, 256.
4. Sobrino, *Where Is God?*, 25.

ing that God's power could not prevail over physical and moral evil, I would rather worship a limited God than an evil one."[5]

In the twentieth-century reflections of rabbi Harold Kushner in *When Bad Things Happen to Good People*, Kushner reflects on the death of his son and asks, "Why do bad things happen to good people?" Kushner questions that common notion of cause and effect based on assumptions of an all-powerful and all-good God.

> The idea that God gives people what they deserve, that our misdeeds cause our misfortune, is a neat and attractive solution to the problem of evil at several levels, but it has a number of serious limitations. As we have seen, it teaches people to blame themselves. It creates guilt even where there is no basis for guilt. It makes people hate God, even as it makes them hate themselves. And most disturbing of all, it does not even fit the facts.[6]

Instead, Kushner comes to an understanding of a limited God who is present with us always, especially in times of suffering. He identifies an open-endedness to creation; a celebration of complexity; an interplay of real relationship between creator and creation and among creatures. Kushner laments suffering and takes it even more seriously by recognizing God impacted by that suffering as well.

Injustice further questions the all-good and all-powerful cohesion. The poorest of the poor and the most vulnerable suffer most. The injustice exposed by natural disasters calls into question the assumption of classical theodicy. Unjust systems intensify randomness and make it more chaotic, producing more suffering. The most vulnerable are not the ones responsible for causing the disaster, but who experience the worst impacts. Their experience disputes a tight causal weave of cause and effect that frames the notions of good and evil, suffering and sin in classical theodicy. Instead, attention to experience in disaster that is rooted in a theology of complex and continuing creation points to a different nature of God. God's nature is not mechanistic but relational.

---

5. Estrada, *Imposible teodicea*, 243.
6. Kushner, *When Bad Things Happen*, 10.

Continuing and Complex Creation

Approaching theology during natural disaster with a lens of creation theology rather than of suffering with the assumption of an all-good and all-powerful God gives credibility to the *kenosis* nature of God. *Kenosis* reinforces a true relationship of trust and love among God and of creation. This creation is continuing and open-ended. It is complex. It is more beautiful than can be imagined. Continuing creation moves the conversation from an abstract God who is all-powerful or all-good to a conversation with God and creation that incorporates mutual accountability. This framework of accountability emerges from, and leads to, actions that practice accompaniment and reinforce the resilience of continuing creativity to embody a whole and flourishing world.

God's Sovereignty and Relationships as Self-Limitation (*Kenosis*)

This open-endedness of complex creation shows a nature of God who not only initiates and enables this process to take place, but participates in it. God is strong enough to practice the self-limitation that enables that process to unfold with the possibility for it always to be more than it is. God's very sovereignty is the self-limitation (*kenosis*) that enables creatures and all of creation to be creative themselves. This authentic creativity brings newness into being. It enables creatures to be what God intends creatures to be and to do.

God and creation are always different. Jürgen Moltmann emphasizes that creation is an act of divine self-definition. "God's determination to be Creator is linked with consideration of the creation that allows it space and time and its own movement, so that it is not crushed by the divine reality or totally absorbed by it."[7] The commitment to communal creation also is a vulnerability for God. Building on this differentiation, Terence Fretheim observes, "The divine relationship to this kind of world is such that God

---

7. Moltmann, "God's Kenosis," 145.

no longer acts with complete freedom but from within a committed relationship to the structures of creation to which God will be faithful."[8] This nature of God's sovereignty also makes possible the reality of suffering and death. Fretheim continues, "This divine constraint and restraint in the exercise of power is a divine commitment that we often wish had not been made, especially when suffering and death are in view. But God will remain true to God's commitments, come what may."[9]

God's creation is composed of interdependent beings and forces. The field of quantum theory gives insight into this complexity. In the early part of the 2000s, John Polkinghorne's compilation of studies at the intersection of science and theology explores quantum theory in relationship to God's self-giving love and creation. The perspective of quantum theory provokes a creation theology that enables disaster theology as complexity to emerge within it. In this volume, Holmes Rolston III positions the relationship between organisms within the creation as interdependent and symbiotic. He observes that the life of every plant or animal is situated within an ecology and life support system. Nothing lives alone. "The individual is immersed in a field of forces transcending its individuality."[10] And further, "The complete set of all causal principles, including human and divine agency, will then be what brings about the future state of the world."[11]

This quantum worldview of creation situates God within the creation and in an immanent relationship with creatures of creation. Catherine Keller, in her process theology, alongside Fretheim's *good not perfect creation* and Moltmann's *creation as kenosis* (see chapter 3) imagines divinity creating from the deep as the Image of God. *Elohim* says "Good!" to everything created, every shining, flowing, glowing, creeping, crawling, swimming,

---

8. Fretheim, *Creation Untamed*, 88.
9. Fretheim, *Creation Untamed*, 16.
10. Rolston, "Kenosis and Nature," 50.
11. Rolston, "Kenosis and Nature," 98.

and finally speaking thing. Good! Good! "God saw everything the he had made, and indeed, it was very good" (Gen 1:31).[12]

Creatures as Co-Creators

Creation is *good*, open to possibilities and open-ended, because immanent and self-giving creativity is the nature of God.[13] God's creatures, therefore, must be agents in creativity ourselves. The nature of God constantly enables just and right relationship. Created and creating in the image of God, therefore, we are beautiful and purposeful and endowed with the potential for participating in right and just relationships ourselves. Development and change built into creation and human vocation help creation to become. "Human words and deeds count; they make a difference to the world and to God, not least because God has chosen to use human agents in getting God's work one in the world."[14]

God shares creative activity by choosing to work with the creation for the very acts of creation. In Job (33:4, 34:14–15, 37:10) already existing creatures are drawn into the creative process. God has tangible and tactile engagement with creatures in the creation story of Gen 2:22–23. Fretheim notes of Gen 2:1–3 that God rests. Human beings do not rest here. In a sense, "God's suspension of creative activity, which allows the creatures, each in its own way, to be what they were created to be . . . God thereby gives to all creatures a certain independence and freedom."[15] Or in a framework of process theology that emphasizes possibilities and becoming, Catherine Keller notes that *Theotopia* needs our invitation to matter, to materialize among us. "We can no longer separate the life that *comes* from our *becoming* lives. This new creation won't happen without our desire, our collusion, our creativity. . . . It is as

---

12. Keller, *Facing Apocalypse*, 130.
13. See chapter 3 for Fretheim's treatment of *good not perfect*.
14. Fretheim, *Creation Untamed*, 15.
15. Fretheim, *Creation Untamed*, 16.

though the messianic always yet to come translates into collective becoming."[16]

That constant change is God's way of equipping each part of creation with the ability to create in its own way; to be constantly creating is what it is to be alive. That constant change means that each part of the reaction has its own free will. It is a co-creator with the Creator and therefore always becoming more than it is already. To cease to become more than it is, is for that creature to die. In other words, a creature must be creator in order to be a full creature. John Polkinghorne and P. J. Hefner, identifying themselves among scientist-theologians, name this "created co-creators."[17]

Recognizing that we are created co-creators reinforces that God is in true relationship with creation. God is really affected by creation: deep grief and exquisite joy and everything on all sides of those relational ties. God can be changed by creation. It is an authentic relationship. It is relationship that can create and transform created co-creators into beauty and purpose that is fuller than can be imagined.

This exploration affirms creation as distinct from the Creator. God also makes the human and the natural world with the true possibility to be co-creators and to become more than the original creation. This is God, therefore, practicing the power of self-limitation and able to be affected, for the sake of authentic right relationship and wholeness for all. The impact of this kind of Creator-Creation relationship is a complex interdependence among creation that can result in natural disasters of disruption and suffering for groups of people. Moral decisions of individuals and societies impact this interdependence and, therefore, the intensity and scope of natural disasters. Actions of response to disasters and preparation for disasters that align with the wholeness of all and of right relationship also follows from this understanding of God's nature.

And, in that, it means that God does continue to act. "God lets the creatures have the freedom to be what God created them

16. Keller, *Facing Apocalypse*, 193.
17. Polkinghorne, "Kenotic Creation," 95. See also Hefner, *Human Factor*.

to be. At the same time, the looseness of the causal weave allows God to be at work in the system in some ways without violating or (temporarily) suspending it. . . . By differentiating self as Creator from a created world, God creates a reality that is not divine but is not Nothing either, and preserves it by distancing self from it."[18]

This differentiation of God from creation while also practicing self-limitation also means that God continually is present and working both within the creation and as more than the creation. This is God's initiative and action for true relationship. The complexity of creation and the interdependence of all parts of creation we experience signals an interdependent nature of God within Godself and corresponding method of creating in collaboration. Such interdependent complexity is another way of identifying the communal character of the cosmos, its basic interrelatedness.

This nature of Creator and creation makes the creation stronger and more resilient. God creates communally so that creation can become what God initiates and with which God is present and active. In other words, this is creation living in the image of God. God gives freedom and independence for each part of creation, and creation as a whole to become the fullness God intends. Fretheim sees in the prophet Isaiah, for example, how God involves human beings in working toward God's goal to heal the environment (Isa 11:1–9, 35:1–10, 65:17–25).[19] In the creative activity, creatures become truly what God intends for them. Creatures cannot become what God intends if God does not allow them to create. And creation cannot become what God intends without creatures as co-creators.

---

18. Moltmann, "God's Kenosis," 137–51. Moltmann traces ideas of *kenosis* prevalent between the seventeenth and twentieth centuries. See this chapter for more on Hebrew *shekinah* as God's indwelling glory present with the exiled people and the Kabbalistic concept of *zimzum* as divine contraction making way for created order. He emphasizes that the God of biblical history is faithful, can repent, and is full of passion and mercy. Therefore, God is not immutable, but can love and can suffer. See also Moltmann, *Theology of Hope* and *Crucified God*.

19. Fretheim, *Creation Untamed*, 7–8.

Authentic Relationship Opens Possibilities for Disaster

The right relationships that God expects and takes extreme action to sustain and to bring into being are those in which actions matter. God is active alongside those who suffer from the disruption of natural disaster in this interdependent creation, affected by those same movements, working always toward just and right relationship. God can also exercise judgment in responding to those actions that intensify the impact and scope of those disasters, sometimes by letting the actions of creation play out to their logical result; sometimes by using other parts of creation as agents; and sometimes by stepping in to change those actions of creation for the sake of those who suffer in order to move the world toward the wholeness of all and mutual love that is right relationship.

Authentic relationship is risky and dangerous. In this authentic relationship with God and creation, every creature will be touched by the movement of every other one, but not in a mechanistic, precise, or inevitable way. This use of creation and creatures in the act of creation itself puts God into authentic relationship with that creation. God needs creation and finds satisfaction in creatures.[20] Our interrelationship is mutually impactful, but it is not a tight causal weave. Fretheim observes,

> Human sin can negatively affect the workings of the natural environment, intensifying already-existing directions of "behavior." Or global warming occasioned by human behaviors may strengthen the workings of storms, making them even more dangerous to the life and health of human beings and animals.[21]

Destruction is also a consequence of this interrelationship. This destruction can manifest in natural disasters. Fretheim acknowledges the destructive consequences of the actions of God and God's co-creators in continuing creation.

---

20. Fiddes, "Creation Out of Love," xiii, 167–91.
21. Fretheim, *Creation Untamed*, 88.

> In the development of such a universe, God chooses to involve that which is other than God, from human beings to earthquakes, tsunamis, periodic extinction of species (over 90 percent to our point in time), volcanic eruptions, and storms galore. All of these creatures of God participate with God in the continuing creation of the universe.[22]

Therefore, the gift of creatures as agents of creativity carries risk. Just as God is strong enough for self-limitation and *kenosis*, so too creatures experience vulnerability and risk. In reflection on the book of Job, Fretheim concludes, "God has chosen not to manage such a world to make sure that no one suffers hurt; God will let creatures be what they were created to be, with all of the potential for creaturely suffering. God has made this creational move for the sake of the fullest life possible."[23] All of this requires mutual accountability toward an outcome of that fullness of life.

God Deliberately Destroys

Complex creation is risky. Creatures and parts of creation often get God's purposes wrong and become destructive whether by intent, limitation, or consequence. Biblical narratives show that God sometimes uses some parts of creation to hold other parts of creation accountable. This can be destructive. In the book of Exodus, God's judgment on human sin is linked with natural catastrophe plagues in Egypt. God's fierce anger is demonstrated through an earthquake that lays a town to ruin in Jer 4:22–26. For God, these acts are deliberate. In Gen 6–9, the biblical emphasis is not on the floods per se, but on the range and intensity of the flood occasioned by human and animal violence.[24] Fretheim observes in Gen 6:11–13 that human and animal violence had the effect of corrupting the earth that God had created. The targeted consequences of

22. Fretheim, *Creation Untamed*, 66.
23. Fretheim, *Creation Untamed*, 89.
24. Fretheim, *Creation Untamed*, 7; Fretheim, "Plagues as Ecological Signs"; Fretheim, "Divine Judgement," 21–32.

such accountability are not in the disaster event itself. "Given the interrelated spiderweb of a world in which we live, every creaturely move affects every other creature, for good or for ill. And human sin intensified the negative effects of this interrelatedness on at least some natural events."[25]

On the other hand, God also uses parts of creation to render surprising encouragement. God speaking to Elijah through a whirlwind in 2 Kgs 2 is such an example. God could have used the whirlwind just as well to wreak disaster to get Elijah's attention. Instead, the whirlwind stirs up God's still small voice to speak to and through the prophet.

The Poor Suffer More

Injustice situated in complex creation eliminates any direct line of cause between the destruction of the disaster and those who suffer. God does not aim disasters at certain communities, but acts do have consequences. Those consequences are not the fair distribution of suffering. Those already in the margins and vulnerable are more susceptible to changes in nature and therefore suffer more. Those without access to resources to prepare for or to recover from disasters suffer more. The poor suffer more.

Disasters may hit everyone, but those without access to resources are impacted most dramatically because those more vulnerable to disruption live in constant disruption and instability. They have less access to recovery assistance and resources. While all in an impacted area of flooding, earthquake, fire, or hurricane may experience that event, the impact on their lives and community is rarely equal. People who are wealthy or settled previously are situated to better withstand the devastating effects of a disaster. People with connections and means already are situated to better recover and rebuild from the disruptions of a disaster. And people with means and power are situated in areas that experience fewer natural disasters with more safety and mitigation structures in

---

25. Fretheim, *Creation Untamed*, 6.

place to experience catastrophes less often or less severe. Natural disasters expose the reality that structural poverty and lack of power were present long before the disaster event impacted communities. Those communities experiencing the worst impacts of disasters were less involved in the factors that caused the event, or its intensified and more frequent occurrence in the first place.

In 2010 Haiti, for example, no direct line exists between those who perished in the destruction of the earthquake and the forces that caused the earth to quake. People who lived in homes that succumbed to the quake suffered because they lived in poverty and were vulnerable to such destruction. Inability to get access to resources for response and recovery because of the social and political history of Haiti dominated by colonial powers and unstable local governments led to more casualties and greater disruption of life.

Climate change in 2024 that causes drought and consequent famine is not caused by those impacted most dramatically. The bulk of greenhouse gases and causes for the intensification and speed of climate change is in nations of the Northern Hemisphere, especially in the United States. The bulk of destructive impacts are in the Southern Hemisphere where people have not even had access to those technologies that have so disrupted the earth. Acts have consequences. Cause and effect are not negated but are more complex than a linear model can conceptualize. Responsibility, blame, and suffering do not coincide.

Holding Each Other and God Accountable

The culmination of authenticity and authority, therefore, is the mutual accountability in which God and creation hold each other. The nature of that accountability is shaped by God who values communal co-creators and who is responsible for complex, open-ended, and continuing creation. God's nature enables the self-correcting and self-limiting dance of true relationships that make all parts of creation accountable to one another. Additionally, if the nature of creation aligns with the nature of God and God is in true relationship with creation, as I believe it does, then God is part of this accountability matrix.

As hard as I tried to not make this a chapter on theodicy, here we are, circling back to an exploration of God's role in disruption, destruction, and evil. So maybe our walk through a creation theology does take us back to the theme of theodicy, but with a twist of holistic well-being and mutual accountability.

Such a complex theodicy holds God accountable to who God is, and to how God creates both from beyond, from within, and with. God creates for the sake of wholeness and well-being. Because God encourages communal agency, when the limitations or (mal)intent of creatures and their systems get in the way of that wholeness, God is accountable. Creatures who participate in the journey of exquisite beauty and the well-being for all also are creatures who cannot be protected from profound disruption (disaster).

Holding God accountable comes out of several trajectories consistent with God's nature and ways of creating. God's being and doing are all for the sake of right relationship of world with God and with each other. The complex causal weave of creation holds all in a weave of mutual accountability and interdependence. Fretheim claims that "we cannot let God off the hook." (1) Natural disasters are an integral part of God's created design. God created a world in which natural disasters were integral to the world's becoming (apart from human behaviors). And (2) natural events may be made more severe by human sin, in connection with divine judgment.[26]

God Suffers with Creation That Suffers: The Nature of Mutual Accountability

So, what is this mutual accountability? The suffering in which God joins the creation in the suffering (in authentic relationship) is key to seeing God's role and nature in actions of continuing creation.

---

26. Fretheim, *Creation Untamed*, 7.

God's Nature Shapes Creation and Its Flourishing

From the lens of disaster, it is in these situations of suffering that I contend this relationship is truly authentic. God suffers with creatures and creation. That relationship is authoritative. God remains present and active for the purposes of transformation and wholeness with those who suffer. It is a relationship that is accountable. Everyone and everything is *all in*. Wholeness and fullness for one part matters for all parts, including for God. It is accountable. God heals from the within as the very nature of Creator as seen in Isa 11:1–9, 35:1–10, or 65:17–25.

God holding creation accountable means that God cares and will not give up. Biblical language for judgment refers to the effects of human sin. Human deeds affect good or ill due to that loose causal weave of act and consequence. Sin has destructive consequences. God is not resigned to evil or tolerant of human sin. God's judgment is for the sake of the well-being and wholeness of the world. This nature of judgment and accountability is the way of suffering and death. "For God to decide to endure a wicked world, while continuing to open up the divine heart to that wicked world, means that God's initially expressed grief is ongoing. God thus determines to take suffering into God's own self and bear it there for the sake of the future of the world."[27]

The assertion that God is embedded in the continuing creation that emerges from the very nature of God as relational situates God as suffering with that creation when it is broken or destroyed. This is not suffering for the sake of suffering, but for the redemption and sustenance of that world of wholeness and flourishing (right relationships). In this way, God is within and beyond creation. God is always making that interconnected beyond a possibility. God is hope (beyond while rooted within). Hope is beyond what can be comprehended or experienced. God is compassion (within while connected beyond). Compassion is deep and moves in and among the strands of relationship. God is community (intertwined, interdependent, and through). Community is the starting place and the ending vision of what can become through this interplay of hope and compassion.

27. Fretheim, *Creation Untamed*, 63.

An understanding of God who only stands outside the disruptions leads only to more disempowerment. Instead, God who is in relationship is love. God loves and wants to be loved. What happens to creation matters. At the same time, using creation as agents in creation itself assures that the process is going to be messy and disorderly. Suffering is going to happen. God remains true to these commitments for true relationship even in the faith of suffering and death. Fretheim agrees, "In the wake of God's initiating activity, God works from within the world rather than on the word from without. . . . And it is that divine decision, for the sake of a very good world, that will occasion much suffering."[28]

This connection changes who God is and what God does. When creatures and creation hurt, God hurts. God suffers with creation. Accountability is built into the very nature of who God is and how God creates. God's suffering with, therefore, is motivation to change and to motivate creatures and creation to change.[29] Suffering is not disaster for the sake of disorder, but suffering for the sake of healing, with creative purpose.

Liturgical Offering: Tumultuous Waters in Art

This stained glass window forms part of the worship space of St. Paul's United Church of Christ in the Missouri River town of Hermann, Missouri. The German immigrants who built the church and chose this photo for one of their stained glass windows knew flooding and other natural disasters. The piety of their tradition may have influenced their choice of pictures for the window. The woman hanging onto the stone cross while waves crash around her might be practicing faith in Jesus over against the chaos of the world she encounters. But another interpretation of this picture puts Jesus right in the heart of the turmoil and chaos of the

---

28. Fretheim *Creation Untamed*, 66.

29. Fretheim *Creation Untamed*, 102. "Indeed, the very relational life of God will have to become engaged in order to restore community and relationships to their rightful place in the world. And then the relational life of God must constitute a model for all of us."

disruptive waters. Jesus as the cross experiences the turmoil as much as any other figure in the scene. Jesus does not lift us out of that chaos but embraces that chaos and weaves a way through.

Stained Glass Window, St. Paul United Church of Christ, Hermann, Missouri.
Photo by author.

Chapter 5

Accompaniment as Proximity and Connection

Personal Microcosm Moments Make Meaning

Covenant of Compassion

MEDIA COVERAGE REVEALED CLARITY. Hurricane Katrina on the Mississippi Gulf Coast and flooding in New Orleans in August 2005 blew open the cover of embedded racism and inequality in those places. Ministries against these injustices are central to the United Church of Christ and our way of being in the world. So, in the wake of the hurricane, communication staff in the UCC's national setting felt compelled to make a strong statement.

I remember well the walls of that office conference room and the table around which staff gathered, anxious to get involved. The magnitude of the impact of the natural disaster of the hurricane and of the human-caused disaster of unequal city infrastructure and government mismanagement gaped open. Staff members speaking most intensely in that room first assumed that the church needed to start from nothing in our response to these disasters. In the energy of the moment, they overlooked the work already in process. They disregarded the already-established relationships for accompanying people in disaster recovery and did not pay attention to ongoing networks in the community organizing against injustice. They were unaware of long-term preparation for this moment that could build on already active processes and institutional relationships. Likewise, the church's actions now could shape disaster recovery and just rebuilding for decades to come.

I was new to the national staff in August 2005 and not at all secure with those more experienced. But I spoke up, advocating that we not create something new but utilize networks and best practices already active. We could activate this moment of clarity to bring theologies and practices of accompaniment into greater public consciousness. I embraced my leadership of collaboration in that moment. Other staff, Florence Coppola, disaster ministries executive, and Susan Sanders, our team leader, filled in the details of those systems already in place and active. Speech in the room halted as everyone listened and began to shape a new and powerful communications strategy.

The *Covenant of Compassion* emerged to sustain the United Church of Christ's role in recovery and rebuilding from Hurricane Katrina for the next decade. One of the smaller players in the recovery, the UCC's influence outsized our numbers because of the way we implemented accompaniment. Many small nonprofit organizations emerged during those years of post-Katrina recovery. They accessed resources and established themselves. Later, many organizations channeled more energy to their organizational self-preservation than to consultation and work alongside local and impacted people.

The *Covenant of Compassion* created a sense of self-accountability in which people who signed the agreement committed themselves to immediate and long-term response as guided by the people impacted by the disaster. The accompaniment approach utilized relationships and already-existing institutional partnerships rooted in long-term commitments of the church. As we watched other organizations flail in attempts to find a way forward on their own, we focused on interacting with people most vulnerable and impacted. We focused on links between those with *unmet needs* and organizations in government and the nonprofit world with resources and experience in disaster recovery.

I remember days and weeks in the fall of 2005 when I communicated directly with thousands of members of the United Church of Christ for whom this disaster and the exposed injustice felt personal. People wanted to act immediately. My response: Bless you and thank you. You are right to be outraged. And the shape of the disaster recovery needs the leadership of those most impacted. It takes some time to get organized. Disaster recovery is long-term. Eventually, the time will be right for your physical action. The denomination will stay close to communicate when those systems are in place. Now is the right time for you to act in solidarity with people in other parts of the country who have experienced previous disaster events and already have response systems in place.

People responded. Powerfully. Groups immediately organized themselves to accompany people in long-term disaster recovery in Florida and in North Dakota. They experienced the importance of remembering people during the long-term of their recovery. Rev. Karen Georgia Thompson, then disaster recovery minister on the Florida Conference of the United Church of Christ staff, helped disaster recovery volunteers see firsthand how the rebuilding work is the longest and most expensive part of recovery.[1] They maintained connections with each other and with disaster ministries of the denomination. When local people on the Mississippi Gulf Coast and in New Orleans were ready to receive their assistance, volunteers went by the thousands, and for years, to accompany survivors of Hurricane Katrina (2005) in their recovery and rebuilding.

This accompaniment approach of solidarity facilitated a methodical response that prioritized local people. It guided significant financial resources and work groups. Networks and connections amplified usually excluded local voices to shape political visibility

---

1. Rev. Karen Georgia Thompson continues to lead in the United Church of Christ. She was elected general minister and president of the denomination in 2023.

and influence that shaped the response and rebuilding beyond the direct influence of the church. Accompaniment and solidarity meant staying for the long-term for many years after Hurricane Katrina occupied the national consciousness. The long-term commitment also shaped younger generations who did not remember the 2005 event but were motivated for new action by participating in the recovery. Accompaniment commitments enabled people to respond to immediate needs and prioritized faith-based advocacy and organizing both locally and nationally.

For ten years following the 2005 disaster event of Hurricane Katrina, UCC volunteer groups received regular correspondence that helped them see the larger context of their housing recovery work in the rebuilding of the communities. The response of solidarity went beyond gutting homes and swinging hammers. It emphasized an active presence, a listening ear so people could tell their stories of trauma and disruption if they needed to talk. And that active presence shifted when people no longer needed to tell their stories to strangers. The active presence reminded impacted people that the world had not forgotten them. Solidarity motivated people to see the ongoing racism and inequality laid bare by the disaster event. People joined social movements or advocated for legislation that addressed root causes of that racism and continued to cause the hurricane's unequal impact in the community. Accompaniment encouraged people around the country to connect the justice issues in New Orleans with those of their own local communities, and to take local action.

Storytelling: New Orleans, Louisiana, December 2005

The empty house. Gutting. We walk into the building three months after Hurricane Katrina and the flood that inundated New Orleans. Walking up to the house, we picked our way over broken glass dotting the front yard. Peeking a head around the wood that once was the door frame, we peered inside. We look around at each other. Where to start? The group divides itself and starts in on the gutting of different rooms. We are entering people's lives. Sacred ground. There are pieces of furniture, waterlogged and then dried, that must be dragged to the curb where trucks will haul it away. Where will all this stuff go? That is the secondary disaster—buried in landfills, in rural areas north in Mississippi or Louisiana, in areas of poverty. The chemicals and poisons of homes when spilled are released into the atmosphere and create an environmental disaster.

I enter the main bedroom. Others start cleaning up the closet in the hallway. Those in the hall drag out moldy blankets, uncovering Christmas decorations that now sit limp, bedraggled, and discolored. Photographs hang on the bedroom walls picturing children and teens, a family growing up, a history. Those photos now sit discolored from water damage five feet high on the wall. So painful. So disorienting. The experience is so disorienting that many people impacted by the disaster feel immobilized and cannot even begin to recover by themselves.

What is the point? The amazing thing of seeing a house gutted down to the studs and frame is the new possibilities that emerge. The family returned to their home while the volunteer group finished cleaning. They walked slowly through the house, gently reaching out to touch a wall where once those family photos hung. Their eyes turned up to look at the ceiling where fans had gently pushed the breeze through the house to mix with babies crying, children laughing, and couples arguing and making up again. A wistful tone filled the room. But hopeful energy emerged. In that open space, the family could see a way forward, could dream about what would come next, and begin to imagine an order to life again.

Disaster Responders as Theologians

My role in natural disasters from 2005 to 2019 focused on creating opportunities for people to engage personally in recovery and rebuilding. Volunteers in groups and as individuals added capacity to response networks that multiplied and leveraged available resources. Volunteer service also created space for personal accompaniment with those impacted by the disaster. The proximity to the dislocation of the disaster and to the strength of survivors enabled personal presence that assured survivors that other people remembered them, offered encouragement, and provided opportunity for storytelling.[2] Disaster recovery volunteers amplified those stories to influence larger systems through organizing and advocacy. I saw firsthand how disaster responders put their faith into action. Theology moves through that faith. The experience shaped theologies with implications throughout life and beyond disaster. I became thoroughly convinced that disaster responders must take seriously their role as theologians.

Because natural disasters are rooted in creation, there is complexity, randomness, patterns, and long-term systems-building. The actions, or inactions of creatures, including humans, impact them. Because response, recovery, rebuilding, and resilience are ways to join God's mission of creating, redeeming, and sustaining, the nature of God matters. Christian theologies amid natural disaster are motivators to accompany those directly impacted. They guide the nature of that journey and relationships of that journey. They point to and move toward the vision of well-being, abundance, and wholeness of God, defining the content of that vision along the way.

"Disaster responder as theologian" is not often the label associated with either side of that simile. And yet, articulating meaning amid disaster's disruption and recovery is work for communities of faith to take seriously. Disasters give the opportunity for—and demand—people of faith to explore what we believe and how we say what we believe in this context, time, and place. People impacted by disaster cope, understand, and build resilience through theological frameworks they have incorporated into their lives before the disruption. Responders from outside who put themselves in proximity to the suffering and destruction also offer important

---

2. Bryan Stevenson, founder and executive director of the Equal Justice Initiative in Montgomery, Alabama, speaks of such commitments as *proximity* to the suffering and marginalized. "Proximity has taught me some basic and humbling truths, including this vital lesson: Each of us is more than the worst thing we've ever done. My work with the poor and incarcerated has persuaded me that the opposite of poverty is not wealth; the opposite of poverty is justice." Stevenson, *Just Mercy*, 17–18.

perspectives on who God is and who we are. Response ministry makes space for people to see God in new ways that takes seriously that experience by involving us in the hard journey that follows, making it our own. Accompaniment marked by relationships of awareness and mutuality form a solidarity that is authentic to the meaning that emerges. Disaster recovery is a meaning-making exercise with implications for the wider community and the whole church. That meaning identifies God's clear presence and helps incorporate people into the very action of God. It seeks justice. This theology discerns the vision of the world for which recovery, rebuilding, and resilience aim. A theological process catalyzed by accompaniment and solidarity is life-giving because it is rooted in authenticity, exercises authority, and utilizes criteria of mutual accountability. The world needs disaster responders to articulate this theology of justice from the place of disaster, for the good of the entire world.

Stay Present: Accompaniment Shapes Theology

Theologies that emerge from acts of accompaniment carry authenticity that changes lives beyond the recovery and rebuilding. That authenticity is rooted in the context of disaster disruptions, and in the personal discernment that comes from that experience. In turn, it shapes the content of that theology.

Destruction Is Real

In Christian tradition, Luke 4:1–13 gives us a window into the importance of Jesus' struggle with the disruption of wilderness. In that wilderness, as his own public ministry was emerging, Jesus struggled with his identity, his style of ministry, and even the definition of God's vision. In Luke 4, he is in the wilderness, a place of isolation, disruption, danger. In this space, the presence of evil makes itself known. Jesus is confronted with social and physical temptations (bread), with temptations of power (authority), and with yearning for security (protection). In each of these temptations, Jesus emerges with a deeper understanding and equipped to practice ministry "with" and "for" the people rather than "over" and "to" them.

Natural disasters, by their very nature, create wilderness. They destroy people's social and physical well-being, property, sense of safety and security. Impacted people often experience a crisis of meaning and purpose. Those outside the impacted area struggle with our relation to God, to one another, and to the nature and style of our ministry in that wilderness.

All of this was so in the aftermath of Hurricane Maria in the fall of 2017 that struck the Atlantic Ocean and Caribbean, including the island of Puerto Rico. Large-scale infrastructure damage and destruction of homes created physical and social hardship (bread). Political and cultural conflicts over who was to respond and how intensified the damage by slowing the immediate response and the beginning of long-term recovery (power). Preexisting economic crises and debt accelerated the displacement of people away from the island and onto the mainland with few resources nor safety nets (protection).

Responses through United Church of Christ and other church organizations took these realities seriously and sought paths to recovery that build a different story. This long-term disaster recovery continues strong. While the public narrative centered on blaming the victims and creating isolationism, the church response emerges from a perspective of Puerto Rican self-determination and accompaniment. People in Puerto Rico need to make decisions for how to recover and need access to resources not available on the island. Therefore, churches on the mainland helped church partners such as the *Iglesia Evangélica Unida de Puerto Rico* (IEUPR) to build their capacity to respond to this disaster. Ongoing connections of those mainland church organizations with government and nongovernment disaster response systems leveraged resources and relationships. One result was that the IEUPR accessed FEMA-provided building materials for homes. Volunteer mission groups from the mainland joined local volunteers and staff to repair and rebuild homes. Local initiatives for solar power in the interior of the island contributed to long-term resilience. Evacuees from Puerto Rico arriving in the mainland accessed support through church coordination of region-wide civic efforts to extend welcome.

In the telling of Jesus' temptation in the wilderness, gospel writers Matthew and Mark end on notes of comfort. Not so in Luke's Gospel. Luke's telling of the story propels Jesus into his public ministry with a foreshadowing of his passion. Disaster recovery in Puerto Rico is long and complex. Perhaps the correspondence with Luke's wilderness story is appropriate. Disaster recovery and accompaniment builds a story of bread, of power, and of protection that is empowering for the people and life-giving for the community.

Connections and Trust

Trust created by authenticity marks that solidarity. For example, following the 2004 tsunami, a Muslim community in Indonesia that previously had experienced Christians only through a narrative of religious conversion, comes to know Christians who want to listen and support them in rebuilding their homes and strengthening their Muslim community. Friendships emerge and shape lives for *the good*. A year later, a flood survivor in North Dakota experiences the hope of a future beyond her destroyed home. Church volunteers from Missouri travel to spend time with her and patiently work with her to sort through soaked belongings. They connect with local North Dakota community resources that help her imagine a path to recovery. Likewise, a homeowner in South Carolina builds back their home with the support of another church disaster responder. Together, they identify a compassion that provides a concrete link between what is and what can be. "These are not just people who talk, but they are doing something," she says. In the response of right relationship, mutual community emerges.

God's Active Presence

In the Jewish tradition, emerging out of her work with rebuilding on the US Gulf Coast following Hurricane Katrina (2005), rabbi Myrna Matsa articulates a Jewish theology of disaster that highlights presence. She notes that Jewish theology of disaster recognizes that good and bad happen in life. "Death and destruction are not signs of life's failure; they are invitations for us to rise to our highest levels of compassion and concern. They provide an opportunity to reach out to each other to provide support, realizing that we cannot take away the devastation, but we can ameliorate it somewhat."[3] Through her disaster recovery experience, Matsa observes that as God is present amid suffering, working from within the devotion to heal, so too, response to the disaster is rooted in a theology of Presence. This divine Presence assures people that they are not forgotten. This divine Presence is calming, not to remove fear, but to lessen isolation. Rabbi Myrna Matsa claims, "To be with a person at a time of need is to honor the survivor's humanity, the inherent dignity endowed by the Creator."[4]

Just Rebuilding: No Longer Excluded Voices

Systemic injustice is part of the story of any disaster. In New Orleans of 2005, those systems displayed themselves fully for the world. The Lower Ninth Ward of New Orleans became a visible and profound story of the racism and classism inherent in the United States and in disaster impact and recovery. Months after the waters receded, I walked through the devastation of the Lower Ninth Ward. The devastation and barrenness took away my breath. Where streets once bustled and homes overflowed with life, now plots lay bare with scattered shells of gutted homes dotting the landscape. Neighborhoods had not come back. Nathaniel Rich of

---

3. Matsa, "Jewish Theology," 4.

4. Matsa, "Jewish Theology," 4. In 2005, Rabbi Matsa served as the rabbinic pastoral/trauma counselor for Hurricane Katrina relief in New Orleans and Baton Rouge, Louisiana, and in the Biloxi/Gulfport, Mississippi, region.

the *New York Times* described the area in 2012, seven years after the storm: "Where once there stood orderly rows of single-family homes with driveways and front yards, there was jungle."[5]

Lower Ninth Ward, New Orleans, Louisiana, December 2006.
Photo by author. Credit Wider Church Ministries, United Church of Christ.

The Lower Ninth Ward of New Orleans had flooded before. It sits in a basin alongside the New Orleans Industrial Canal that connects the Mississippi River and Lake Pontchartrain. Extensive canal dredging to support commercial development had diminished the surrounding wetlands and made the area more prone to flooding. In 2005, former residents of the Lower Ninth Ward raised suspicion that water management decisions, not only the storm surge itself, caused the levees to breach and break here. Water entered the Lower Ninth Ward from three sides, two of them levee breaches. The decision relieved pressure on the levees at other locations, preventing even more massive flooding in parts of the city more affluent and more white. The suspicions had precedent. A levee on the Industrial Canal collapsed in 1965 during Hurricane Betsy, flooding the area and delaying recovery, also surfacing suspicions about water management decisions based on race and economic influence. In 2005, the Lower Ninth Ward of New Orleans had one of the highest rates of black homeownership

---

5. Rich, "Jungleland."

in the nation.[6] In the early 1900s, the city sold lots inexpensively to African American families. People built homes and created neighborhoods. Jobs were available in the surrounding shipping and commercial sectors.[7] Families passed their homes from generation to generation. So many generations of home ownership ensued that deeds to homes and land were lost. Other deeds had not been formally transferred to inheritors or named multiple people. Some were destroyed in the flood. By 2005, people in the Lower Ninth Ward owned their homes, but many lived in poverty. Jobs, transportation, and education had moved away. Following the hurricane, many people were denied access to resources to recover and rebuild because they could not produce deeds to their homes as evidence of ownership. Other resources for recovery were limited or made difficult to access. Community cleanup and services did not return to the neighborhoods. The displacement sparked outrage at first as the world watched through television cameras the devastation of the levee break. But then silence. And eventually forgetting. Within a few years, plans for civic green space began to replace efforts to rebuild neighborhoods. Within a decade, new condominium developments in the area reinforced the gentrification of New Orleans preferencing white millennials with economic resources as new homeowners. Neighborhoods denied. Injustice revealed and then ignored and exacerbated.

The magnitude of disaster recovery and its failures in the Lower Ninth Ward of New Orleans testifies to the importance of paying attention to excluded voices as the criteria for successful *just rebuilding*. Rebuilding with justice not only exposes inequities and broken systems active before the disaster but changes those systems so this human-caused disaster does not take place again.

This commitment to *just rebuilding* can take root in a theology of disaster centered in the liberation goal expressed in John 10:10, *life in all its fullness*. "I came that they may have life and have it abundantly." It recognizes that people who experience the most disruptive effects of natural disasters are the most excluded,

6. Breckenridge-Jackson, "Preserving History."
7. Mwendo and Plyer, "Beyond Data."

oppressed, and vulnerable both before and following the event. Listening to their voices to define *abundant life* then is the authority for the nature and focus of *just rebuilding*. A liberation lens for theologies of disaster asserts that injustice is not deterministic or preordained. Injustice is the result of deliberate ways humans organize our society with the tether of power rather than the goal of abundance for all. Injustice as human-caused tragedy accentuates natural disasters by intensifying the speed and frequency of climatic changes to cause more disruption. Systems of injustice make more excluded people more vulnerable to the impacts of those changes. The cycle continues to accelerate. Natural disasters expose injustice.

Without a Lens of Just Rebuilding Injustice Intensifies

Against "Clean Slate" Recovery

Disasters further exclude people when those in power practice "clean slate" recovery. When a natural disaster causes catastrophic damage, older housing disappears. The landscape appears like a *clean slate*. The public narrative might be building back better, but those who experienced the disaster rarely benefit. Gentrification or higher housing costs often double displace people who can no longer afford to live there. Commercial zoning changes prevent people from returning home.

Again, following Hurricane Katrina in 2005, casinos in Biloxi, Mississippi, practiced *clean slate* recovery. Before the disaster, local ordinances prevented casinos from building on land. Casinos operated on large barges on the bay. At a public hearing one month after the storm, public officials claimed, "The big question was not whether, but where to rebuild the huge casinos that have made the region the country's third largest casino market."[8] The storm surge had lifted one of those barges and deposited it on an apartment building where people perished. The barge remained wrecked there for many months, symbolizing the need (casino owners and

---

8. PBS News Hour, "Mississippi Approves," para. 1.

government officials claimed) to change local ordinances to not only allow, but require, casinos be built on land. Republican Governor Haley Barbour asserted, "You've seen the catastrophic destruction of the casinos and the destruction wrought by those behemoths when they crashed into buildings and vehicles. We can't return the casinos to the way they were. It would be irresponsible."[9]

Biloxi, Mississippi, post-Hurricane Katrina, August 2005.
Photo by Shari Prestemon. Credit Back Bay Mission.

The community response was mixed. Casinos were the first businesses to rebuild and restart. They helped the economic regeneration of the region. In the short term, they provided jobs. But the casinos solidified an economic stratification in the community. Housing prices soared as the casinos' profit expanded. People worked available part-time jobs but could not afford to live nearby. As casinos increasingly hired people outside of Biloxi, those who lost homes lost livelihoods, too.

Instead, Back Bay Mission, a community ministry of the United Church of Christ in Biloxi, leaned into relationships that had been developed in the community for a century to prioritize housing recovery for those most excluded. Back Bay Mission, led

9. PBS News Hour, "Mississippi Approves," para. 5.

by then-executive director Rev. Shari Prestemon, gathered resources and coordinated groups of volunteers and individual long-term volunteers to interact with local people most impacted by the tsunami and accompany them in home repair and rebuilding the community.[10] That work together continues to this day.

Back Bay Mission, Biloxi, Mississippi, September 2005.
Photo by Shari Prestemon. Credit Back Bay Mission.

10. Rev. Shari Prestemon continues to lead in the United Church of Christ. In 2024, she began serving as the acting associate general minister of the national United Church of Christ and co-executive of global ministries (Christian Church Disciples of Christ/United Church of Christ).

Accompaniment as Proximity and Connection

Back Bay Mission, Biloxi, Mississippi, September 2005.
Photo by Shari Prestemon. Credit Back Bay Mission.

Back Bay Mission, Biloxi, Mississippi, 2009.
Photo by author. Credit Wider Church Ministries, United Church of Christ.

A similar "clean slate" recovery with casinos at the heart emerged years later in the Philippines after Typhoon Haiyan in 2013. Waves and wind destroyed the informal settlements of fisher people. Families built these villages so they could be close to the coast as the source of their fishing livelihood. They did not, however, own the land. When the storm wiped the coast clean, landowners took the opportunity to prevent their return. Fisher people found themselves landless and homeless. Those who were able to return to fishing hauled their boats over land long distances. Others lost their livelihoods as well. Soon casinos and resorts appeared on those coastlines.

The United Church of Christ in the Philippines drew on its experience in advocacy honed unfortunately by many years of protesting injustices including land rights. They organized to stand with these fisher people to reclaim the land on which they previously lived. Disaster recovery became as much about political action as about hammers and nails. Advocates for landrights joined advocates for climate justice in public rallies and in the courts.

United Church of Christ in the Philippines, post-Typhoon Haiyan, 2013. Photo by Zach Wolgemuth. Credit Wider Church Ministries, United Church of Christ.

Accompaniment as Proximity and Connection

United Church of Christ in the Philippines, post-Typhoon Haiyan, 2013. Photo by Zach Wolgemuth. Credit Wider Church Ministries, United Church of Christ.

The "clean slate" pattern of recovery repeats again and again. Hurricane Maria devastated Puerto Rico in 2018. Economist Naomi Klein calls out northern off-island entrepreneurs who move in to profit from new solar power stations even as a decades-long paucity of economic opportunities has driven younger generations to the mainland United States. She names the situation *Puertopia* in her book, *The Battle for Paradise: Puerto Rico Takes on Disaster Capitalists*.[11] In an inside cover review of Klein's book, 2017 San Juan mayor Carmen Yulin Cruz claims that the path to equality and sustainability is driven by communities, not investors. "Only community activists can answer the paramount question, 'What type of society do we want to become and who is Puerto Rico for?'"

---

11. Klein, *Battle for Paradise*. The essay from Puerto Rico rises from Naomi Klein's more expansive work to expose disaster capitalists by examining war, terror, economic warfare, and regime change as disaster. See Klein, *Shock Doctrine*.

Unequal Access to Resources, Unequal Recovery

Marginalized people are the most severely impacted by disaster because they are vulnerable and living in dangerous places already. The recovery also can further marginalize people through unequal access to resources for rebuilding or be the excuse for deliberate exclusion.

Jonathan M. Katz, an American journalist, lived in Haiti at the time of the 2010 earthquake. As his house buckled from the earthquake, he began to observe the response and recovery firsthand. In his book *The Big Truck That Went By: How the World Came to Save Haiti and Left Behind a Disaster*, Katz critiques international aid and good intentions gone wrong.[12] He notes large donations by people in the United States but does not see more safe housing or fewer people living in poverty in Haiti. Haitians did not direct their own recovery. Katz's observations expose the way the United States government distributes international aid in times of disaster. Monies put toward recovery finance the United States military itself to do the work, effectively providing an internal funding stream. Katz recognizes that this military presence also exerts control in a region for defense purposes, contributing to the colonial relationship existing from the transatlantic slave trade to the present turmoil. Haiti remains the poorest nation in the Western Hemisphere. The book cover of *The Big Truck That Went By* pictures a little girl sitting on a barren hillside, watching US military transport trucks travel on the dirt road below. Her body language signals detachment as if the trucks moving through her space make no difference in her world. She continues to live in poverty the earthquake made more dire.

On the other hand, prioritizing the leadership of people impacted by the disaster for their own recovery leads to different engagement and different outcomes. While many recovery organizations and governments set up their own shops to do disaster recovery for Haiti following the massive 2010 earthquake, the United Church of Christ and Fuller Disaster Rebuilders intentionally put

---

12. Katz, *Big Truck*.

resources and experience at the service of Haitian communities for long-term recovery. As they camped out in makeshift villages created from blue FEMA-provided tarps, Haitian community leaders identified housing as a priority. But they expressed caution. These leaders had seen other outside groups make decisions that boded poorly for people's long-term well-being. They watched multiple houses emerge on arid land, probably easy to procure, constructed of four thin walls and a makeshift roof. The local leaders knew this was not sustainable, not least of all because the organizations had not considered sanitation before choosing their construction site and house model. This partnership instead started with latrines. Eventually construction moved to substantive walls and roofs. They determined sites for houses located near markets. Accessible roads connected people to services and enabled transportation of goods to sell for livelihoods. Soon, local economies with corner food carts started again. Eventually, schools and clinics emerged in the area. People planned and rebuilt their own community. The process was life-giving at many levels. Dignity, hopes, and dreams budded.

Homes in Haiti, post-2010 earthquake.
Photo by author. Credit Wider Church Ministries, United Church of Christ.

Joining God in the Thin Places

Homes in Haiti, post-2010 earthquake.
Photo by author. Credit Wider Church Ministries, United Church of Christ.

Homes in Haiti, post-2010 earthquake.
Photo by author. Credit Wider Church Ministries, United Church of Christ.

Accompaniment as Proximity and Connection

Disasters Expose Systemic Injustice Before, During, and After

Liberation theologian Jon Sobrino of Central America[13] emphasizes how disaster exposes ongoing realities of injustice and inequality. He sees his theological reflections on "Christology at a crossroads" and "crucified peoples" embodied in the people of El Salvador after catastrophic earthquakes in early 2001. Sobrino laments, "The earthquake is not just a tragedy, it is an X-ray of the country."[14]

El Salvador is situated in a disaster-prone part of the North American continent. The January 13, 2001 earthquake that created widespread destruction followed other massive earthquakes in 1965 and in 1986. It followed frequent hurricanes, including named storms Hurricane Fifi in 1974 and Hurricane Mitch in 1999. Since 2001, El Salvador has experienced dozens of earthquakes and over twenty-four named hurricanes or tropical storms. Jon Sobrino observes that decades of acute repression, war, destruction, massive emigration, and migration operate on top of the everyday poverty and injustice active in the country. This combination prevents full recovery from any of these natural disasters or human-caused tragedies.

Sobrino confirms that the January 2001 earthquake caused initial injuries, death, and destruction. Homes built of mud, sticks, and adobe, because people cannot afford cement and iron, crumble more readily than other homes. Floods and mudslides bury people

---

13. Jon Sobrino, SJ, is author of several central texts in Christian liberation theology in the late twentieth and early twenty-first centuries. Sobrino served as Jesuit Roman Catholic priest in El Salvador. His publications include *Christology at the Crossroads* (1978), *The True Church and the Poor* (1984), *Spirituality of Liberation* (1990), *Jesus the Liberator* (1991), *The Principle of Mercy: Taking the Crucified People from the Cross* (1994), *Christ the Liberator* (1999), and *No Salvation Outside the Poor* (2008). Sobrino was away on travel when a unit of the Salvadoran Army murdered his six fellow Jesuits, their housekeeper, and her daughter on November 16, 1989. The Army targeted these Jesuits for their outspoken work for peace to bring resolution to the Salvadoran Civil War.

14. Sobrino, *Where Is God?*, 3.

who live in poverty because the steep and barren hillsides are often the only places they are allowed to plant crops. In the days following an earthquake, people not only experience distress of their uncertain future of survival and anxiety about getting the credit needed to rebuild their houses and lost livelihood. There is always the additional fear that the earth might start trembling again. And it does. "So, to live in El Salvador is a heavy burden, but it is not borne equally by everyone."[15]

Ines Che and Caterina, El Salvador, January 2024. Photo by author.

15. Sobrino, *Where Is God?*, 2.

Accompaniment as Proximity and Connection

Author and Caterina, El Salvador, January 2024.
Photo by Kurt Schaller Blaufuss.

Joining God in the Thin Places

El Salvador Volcano, January 2024. Photo credit by author.

Even as Sobrino analyzes earthquakes in his nation of El Salvador, he laments the lack of attention the rest of the world gives to mitigating the next natural disaster. The next disaster is not a surprise. He notes that catastrophic earthquakes occur every fifteen or twenty years in Central America, but the politicians, government officials, soldiers, oligarchs, even the international community of opulence never seem to learn from the ensuing tragedy. No one does anything effective to avoid or minimize, as far as possible, the next tragedy.

People living in poverty experience even deeper destitution after a disaster impacts them. Setting safety standards for housing construction has no impact when no possibility exists that people could comply. The standards themselves, therefore, become an insult. Deforestation that exaggerates mudslides continues to harm the environment. Yet people with no other choices continue to build houses in the path of such destruction. Sobrino speaks of the tragedy of one of those mudslides. Months before the 2001 earthquake, contractors built houses in the deforested areas of the Bálsamo Mountains. People demonstrated against the construction with posters and banners because of the danger posed by the barren hillsides. The construction continued anyway. People with no other housing occupied the structures. As the earth quaked, mudslides began and destroyed the village. Sobrino's breaking point came when rescuers dug a little girl's body out of the ruins with one of those protest banners in her hands. The destruction of the mudslide seemed unbearable.[16] Injustice compounds with each tragedy when nothing is done to prevent or minimize the negative impact of the next disaster. A decade later, following the August 2021 hurricanes that struck El Salvador, little had changed as church partners of Global Ministries (Christian Church Disciples of Christ/United Church of Christ) made similar observations about environmental degradation, exclusion, and poverty.[17] During my own visit to El Salvador in January 2024 I met Ines Che and Caterina, who regularly evacuate their homes and farms for flash floods with waters chest high. The only lands available to them are in the path of these frequent floods, at the epicenter of the 2001 earthquake, and without access either to electricity or sewer systems that support anything but an outhouse for a latrine. Disasters disproportionately impact people without access to resources and those least responsible for climate change accelerating extreme weather events.

And yet, as those systemic injustices are exposed, the voices of those excluded give us vision of goals for recovery and rebuilding. Sobrino tells those of us not immediately impacted to stay present in the suffering of people who experience destruction. Sobrino names this solidarity "praxic theodicy." It includes

> (1) indignation in response to human suffering, acknowledging there is something irremediable about suffering (2) hope that God—whether or not God has the power to overcome suffering—does have the power to nurture human hope (3) honesty to take charge of a horrible reality and to take responsibility for it. "Praxic theodicy" includes the decision to practice justice and kindness and to walk humbly with God through history, in the darkness, protesting as we go, but always going.[18]

---

16. Sobrino, *Where Is God?*, 4.
17. Global Ministries, "Disasters in Central America."
18. Sobrino, *Christ the Liberator*, 143.

Thus, the motivation for my own visit of accompaniment in early 2024. Sobrino names the suffering people the "crucified people."[19] He challenges us to let ourselves be affected by the tragedy and not turn away or soften it. That presence leads to solidarity, compassion, and assistance. It leads to the "miracle of holding each other up, of giving and receiving the best that we have. And the even greater miracles of loving one another as members of one family."[20]

---

19. Sobrino expands on the theology of "crucified people" beginning in the 1990s in *Crucified Peoples*. See also Sobrino, *Principle of Mercy*.

20. Sobrino, *Where Is God?*, 9.

Chapter 6

Solidarity Seeking Justice

Personal Microcosm Moments Make Meaning: Discernment and Negotiation in Global Community Development

I BELIEVE THAT DISASTER responders make good theologians. In 2013, I was struggling with the role of the church in relation to government grants for *Just Rebuilding*. Maybe the church should go alone on our limited scale. A colleague convinced me otherwise.

It was my first meeting to represent the United Church of Christ with the organization of churches, IMA World Health. IMA World Health is a national organization through which churches in the United States join communities around the world to address public health challenges. Projects of the organization seek to improve nutrition, strengthen health systems, and improve maternal and child health. IMA World Health had been active for many years in the HIV/AIDS crisis.[1]

The organization works cooperatively with several United Nations agencies as well as local governments. We boarded a bus to travel to a restaurant for the committee's evening meal. I sat

---

1. IMA World Health, https://imaworldhealth.org/.

with Gretchen and, for some reason, felt empowered to proclaim my opinion. Some of the discussion at coffee breaks during the day's meeting concerned a different organization that had accepted United States government contracts for road building in Afghanistan. When the funds of that grant ran out the organization left those roads half-completed and unusable by local people for trade or other communications. I joined the skepticism that ruled the room that morning in that it seemed when the stretch of road needed by the US military was complete, the promise to the local people of a larger road network may have been deemed unnecessary. Why would IMA World Health involve itself with government grants when they might have such a hidden agenda? Gretchen looked at me, silently at first. She was originally from East Berlin, so a German accent to her English along with a strong look of experience in economic uplift on her face impressed me. "We don't apply for every government grant," she responded. "Only those that fit OUR vision." Of course. That interaction still guides me. "Wise as serpents and innocent as doves" (Matt 10:16). Thank you, Gretchen. No response and recovery effort will be totally altruistic at every level. And, embedded good persists. Resources exist to piece together for the good. The question is to be clear about our vision. What is good; for whom; who decides and how? To me, this is the theological process that is ongoing and dialogical. It needs to be community, guided by the criteria of the well-being of the most excluded or vulnerable.

Getting Systems to Work for the Good

In light of the authority of those most marginalized for their well-being, we must always be reexamining mechanisms of response, recovery, and rebuilding. We need to be aware of, understand, and access current response and recovery mechanisms. But we do not accept those processes as they exist without question.

Jesus' parable and instruction to his disciples to stay alert, to be "wise as serpents and innocent as doves" (Matt 10:16), indicates he is preparing his followers to be in the world but not of it; to always have a theological lens tuned toward the good. What pieces of the power structure can be used toward a goal of equity and what needs to be resisted? That goal of equity could be named redemption. Redemption, as in creation, is continuing. It is a process. It is a process that is interconnected and interdependent, not linear. Redemption is a process that adapts and bends and waves. The process requires continual interpretation to determine the vision of abundance, wholeness, and fullness of life from the perspective of those who currently live as excluded or who suffer. Redemption as "just rebuilding" requires constant discernment and negotiation to change current mechanisms to work for that good.

I learned these lessons of discernment and negotiation through engagement with disaster response and recovery organizations both in the United States and globally. The continual challenge—listening to and learning from those whose voices have been excluded.

One way some approach changing systems is to ignore or find a way around existing structures. I observed this approach during the Hurricane Katrina recovery on the Mississippi Gulf Coast after the 2005 disaster. Many people wanted to assist in the recovery. Funds were available for organizations. The phenomenon of pop-up disaster response organizations emerged. Organizations with no connection to wider networks or to local people suddenly appeared. The stories followed a similar trajectory. A new organization raised money for their infrastructure and projects. They accessed grants and received individual donations. Work began. Sometimes the organization hired local people to implement the project. Usually the organization's decision-makers had no roots in the local community, nor tried to connect locally in any substantive way. Without communication or cooperation among the organizations, they competed among each other rather than listen to the most vulnerable people in the communities. Lots of time and energy was used to negotiate territory and visibility. Few of these pop-up organizations survived long-term. Those that could not continue often left projects unfinished. I learned from this negative experience the importance of coordination, cooperation, and partnerships.

Public-Private Partnerships Are Global and Local

The disaster response world within the United States and around the world is a complex system of public-private partnerships. Even within the United States, governments at various levels cooperate. County emergency management systems and FEMA each serve a particular role in a disaster response. Voluntary organizations connect with each other and these public entities through networks such as the National Voluntary Organizations Active in Disaster (NVOAD), State Voluntary Organizations Active in Disaster (VOADs), and Community Organizations Active in Disaster (COADs). The American Red Cross is a private organization with special contracts with FEMA to act as an agent of the government in some disaster situations. Globally, national governments each have their mechanisms of action. Civil society has organized itself through agencies of the United Nations and other international nongovernmental organizations.

Those systems identify and channel resources as learned in previous responses. Already-established organizations have access to power and resources; financial donations, people with expertise in coordination, in construction, in psychosocial care. Established systems involve people who have spent lifetimes learning and working and learning from others to implement effectively. They have access to resources and can operate at scale to combine expertise in logistics with research such as the continuum of a disaster developed by NVOAD[2] or the latest research in climate change.

Large systems also can take on a life of their own. Mechanisms can appear technical and practical rather than relational. Government organizations such as FEMA might have a mandate for disaster recovery, but the systems may not preference the most vulnerable. Relationships among the organizations meant

2. National Voluntary Organizations Active in Disaster, https://www.nvoad.org/.

to facilitate cooperation and multiplied effectiveness may not be flexible enough to adapt to changing situations. Organizations with experience and scope have established procedures, protocols, and parameters in which they operate. Those operations focus on effective ways to implement recovery and rebuilding. But customization for different types of responses may fall outside those norms. The tone of large-scale disaster recovery presents itself as technical and complex.

Communities of Faith Have Impact

Navigating access to these large systems and shaping those responses for the benefit of normally excluded people takes its own expertise. Faith communities, including churches, have a distinct role to play. They help fill gaps, leverage resources, and bring measures of accountability to the process. Faith communities bring local and excluded voices to the criteria of what constitutes recovery. Many faith communities have organized to leverage resources and increase capacity through cooperation. Global organizations in the ACT Alliance are activated for humanitarian response to bring government and collective resources to the service of local communities. Relationships among organizations are important to lead to collaboration and cooperation and mutual influence and multiplied effectiveness These mechanisms each have their particular role and bring the experience of response in other disasters and in other locations to the service of the response at hand. National governments of some of these organizations in Europe recognize them as formal humanitarian responses of those governments while the church organizations in other parts of the world operate independently of national governments. These faith-based organizations with national and global scope have access to resources and can operate at scale to combine expertise in logistics with research such as the continuum of a disaster.

International faith communities accompanied the people of Nepal, for example, following a catastrophic earthquake in April 2015. The Himalayan Mountains shook as tectonic plates shifted.

Homes and communities tumbled. People have few resources and homes are poorly built. Nepal has few resources as a nation for massive rebuilding. People died. Ongoing and long-lasting political turmoil and violence reflect and create social instability. Nepal's closed government is suspicious of outside groups. As a Hindu government, it is especially dubious about outside religious groups.

The situation may have presented itself as easier for the rest of the world to go about our business and let the Nepalese deal with this tragedy on their own. Why bump up against international boundaries and cultural expectations? But the world did take notice. As part of global church disaster agencies with global credibility of technical expertise and insistence on serving all, a particular denomination such as the United Church of Christ with which I worked could be part of immediate and long-term response through these organizations already in place in Nepal. Seeking partnerships of organizations serving globally with skills in housing construction, the UCC supported the construction of fifty earthquake-resistant homes. As participants in the 2015 global Paris Climate Summit, the UCC could help influence attitudes and international norms to address climate change that continues to destabilize the environment of the mountainous Himalayan region of Nepal. Nepal does not headline the global news, but communities know they are not forgotten when international faith communities journey alongside them as they rebuild their lives and communities.

In the United States, churches are national in scope through denominational disaster offices. Denominations and groups of denominations such as Church World Service exert influence on local, state, and federal levels to increase access to resources and to leverage those resources toward the most vulnerable. Collective action by churches influences the insurance industry toward greater responsibility. And where gaps exist in government and private resources, these national churches connect with other church responses and with other voluntary organizations to meet impacted people with volunteer action and resources. Their cooperation and coordination avoid duplication of services and multiply the special assets of each denomination.

The values inherent in secular and government response organizations have been influenced heavily by the values emerging from communities of faith. Part of this is keeping emotional and spiritual care integral to recovery. Spiritual care in disasters also supports research that has emerged in the continuum of recovery that puts an emphasis on the long-term nature of rebuilding (see image below).[3]

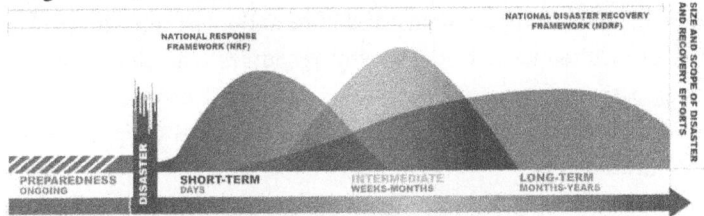

FEMA Long-Term Recovery Continuum

In large-scale disasters that garner media attention, the spotlight often is turned to the recovery and immediate response, but the long-term rebuilding actually is the costliest and the most impactful part of that aftermath. In small-scale disasters or in locations when media attention is absent, attention is still needed for this long-term recovery. The "four Cs" advocated by the National VOAD as best practices—Cooperation, Communication, Coordination, and Collaboration—all are directly rooted in faith traditions.[4]

At the same time, the church is local. Churches often offer their buildings as emergency shelters for those impacted or housing for volunteer groups engaged in recovery. And communities trust local leaders whom they know. Leaders build community relationships that coordinate locally through long-term recovery organizations. Churches help access resources for the sake of their local community's recovery—linking networks and resources

---

3. FEMA, "Recovery Continuum."
4. NVOAD, *Light Our Way*, 2.

available in these secular and government organizations, as well as in the ecumenical community.⁵

Janice Howe served as pastor of Third Congregational Church of Alstead, a small church of the United Church of Christ in rural New Hampshire. When the town flooded in October 2005, members of her congregation and the wider community looked to the church for spiritual care and emotional support. She officiated funerals and coordinated community meetings. The church connected with state and national resources through denominational ties. She preached persistence and hope and interpreted for people the FEMA sequence of delivery of resources. The church served as an active presence for long-term recovery. Howe recorded her learnings in a book, *Nothing Ever Happens Here: A Guide to Disaster Ministry*.⁶

The global and connectional identity of church communities and the motivation to be God's hands and feet in the world, being redeemed and made whole create a network for effective implementation of such lifesaving and sustaining methods. International institutions such as the United Nations and secular conversations once skeptical of religious institutions, seeing religious identity as getting in the way of holistic recovery rather than making it more effective, are paying more attention to religious institutions that operate from a liberation theological framework. They are a counter to perceived religious fundamentalist institutions. In a sense, the networks of church that are part of that theological emphasis on relationship and a belief that God is working in the world and that humans and creation are agents in that work as well as recipients—are a ready-made system for movements. Church congregations are local hubs of influence with trusted leaders within local communities. These local hubs have global connections and faith-based organizations are often operated from a position of

---

5. Gopp and Gilvin, *Help and Hope*.

6. Howe, *Nothing Ever Happens Here*. The Alstead, New Hampshire, disaster experience impacted the entire Howe family. In 2023, Katie Howe, Janice's daughter, began serving on the national United Church of Christ staff as minister for disaster response and recovery.

compassion rather than of self-interest. This multilayered presence and its effectiveness offer the space for those involved to be taken seriously in the theological dialogue in which we engage.[7]

Filling Gaps and Leveraging Influence

The accountability of solidarity seeking justice prioritizes the most vulnerable. In places where the rules of other organizations require certain ways of using funds or certain personal criteria to be met, response guided by accompaniment and solidarity operates differently. The accountability of *just rebuilding* prioritizes local leaders and vulnerable voices. It encourages capacity building to share expertise and grow resilience. The accountability of those on the margins as primary actors motivates changes to systems that work toward their marginalization no longer. Influences on complex disaster response systems of the government, insurance, secular organizations create change at scale. And rebuilding with justice is systemic and long-term.

Capacity Building in the Philippines, 2013–2017

Building capacity to respond to the next disaster while responding to the current crisis is also a mark of accountability for equitable recovery. Communities build resilience. In the Philippines, following Typhoon Haiyan in 2013, United Church of Christ members and friends responded with abundance. UCC Disaster Ministries connected with the United Church of Christ in the Philippines (UCCP) long-time partner church of Global Ministries (Christian Church Disciples of Christ/United Church of Christ). The UCC Philippines has a long history of speaking as the poor, demanding equality, and justice. These disaster rebuilding efforts fit the same pattern. The church responded immediately to displaced fisher families with boats and to farmers with seed. Typhoon Haiyan's

---

7. This approach of global civil society organizations is expanded upon in World Council of Churches and ACT Alliance, *Called to Transformation*.

destruction and the ongoing injustice in society, lamentably, made the crisis more complex. So, in that immediate response, the church looked to the long term. Decisions on how to rebuild immediately engaged issues of land rights. Homes were planned and rebuilt to not only offer shelter for the present, but to resist future storms. Knowing that future typhoons will likely hit the islands of the Philippines as climate change increases the intensity and frequency of large storms, the UCCP created its own office of disaster ministries. The UCCP regularly shares expertise with others in the Philippines and other parts of the region and world through this increased capacity.

Initiating Change: Renters in Texas, 2017

Providing expert accountability and inside pressure to larger organizations shapes the disaster response toward equity. Filling these gaps then influences larger secular and government mechanisms to prioritize the most vulnerable. How to work with renters is one part of disaster recovery in the United States continually in negotiation. Private and volunteer response organizations normally avoid assistance with structures that landlords rent to others. The owner of the rebuilt structure still owns that property. They are not required to assure that the original renter can return. Landlords with a nicer structure and perhaps a *clean slate* neighborhood recovery likely increases rental charges. Low-income renters cannot return. Yet many of the most vulnerable and marginalized people impacted by disasters in the United States rent. Renters experienced this in New Orleans after 2005's Hurricane Katrina. Landlords repeatedly utilized insurance coverage payouts to upgrade their properties and then outprice their tenants. In post-Katrina New Orleans, gentrification accelerated so that original residents of the city could no longer afford to live there. Neither could many of those who were mass evacuated from the city during the days of the hurricane event and subsequent flooding afford to return. Many created lives for themselves, or experienced difficulties in so doing so, in other locations around the country.

An initiative by NVOAD with United Church of Christ leadership in 2017 experimented with a way to address this difficult situation with more justice for renters. Following Hurricane Harvey, which caused widespread destruction in Houston and surrounding areas of Texas in 2017, UCC Disaster Ministries connected with people again left out of the spotlight of that recovery. In Jefferson County, the communities of Beaumont and Port Arthur near the coast received widespread destruction but very little attention for recovery. Local leaders of the Southeast Texas Community Development Corporation (SETCDC) had been active in the area for many years providing affordable housing for renters. This nonprofit organization owned properties in the area with the goal to support and revitalize their struggling community. The storm damaged multiple houses of the SETCDC along with other homes in the area rented by people with lower incomes. People had no place to go. Through a partnership in Jefferson County, Texas, UCC Disaster Ministries and SETCDC leadership committed to help lower-income renters get back into their homes. They also committed to help people priced out of other houses find an affordable home to rent. The organizations shared learnings with other churches and voluntary organizations nationally to add possible models for equitable disaster recovery for people with the least access to resources.

Solidarity Seeking Justice

Disaster response, recovery, and rebuilding accomplished through accompaniment and solidarity for the goal of justice is authentic in its relationships. It embodies the authority of those most devastated. It exercises accountability that is life-giving. These are high aspirations, and we are people mired in limitations and embedded in complex systems difficult to change. In reality, responses may not be effective. Recovery efforts may miss the mark of equity. Rebuilding may not be able to guide every response mechanism into justice. Repentance, therefore, is integral to theologies in the thin places of natural disaster. That repentance relates to the vision of fullness of life envisioned by those who suffer most from the destruction of disasters. Jon Sobrino's *praxis theodicy* (see chapter 5) reminds us to stay present and remain indignant at suffering, to know that God has the power to nurture human hope amid suffering, and to take responsibility for horrible realities. Sobrino encourages us in the decision "to practice justice and kindness and to walk humbly with God through history . . . protesting as we go, but always going."[8]

---

8. Sobrino, *Christ the Liberator*, 270. See also Sobrino, *Where Is God?*, 9.

Chapter 7

Community Resilience

Personal Microcosm Moments Make Meaning: Life Will Find a Way

OF ALL THE BOARDS of trustees on which I have served, A Christian Ministry in the National Parks (ACMNP) is one of my favorites. Being a national park enthusiast myself, I was encouraged to be with others who also found inspiration in the natural beauty of God's creation. ACMNP provides leadership for Christian (ecumenical) worship services in the parks and provides a ministry of presence among visitors and summer staff to help appreciate God's good creation and one another. Leadership development is integral as the agents of this work are college-aged young adults. A perk of being on the national advisory board of ACMNP is that meetings take place in one of the US National Parks. In those parks, creative processes are out in the open. One can experience the opposites of extremes of magnificence and empty desolation right in your face.

Glacier National Park is this mix of awe and terror. In this park, the majesty of mountains is augmented by mountain sheep precariously, but sure-footedly, making their way along steep craggy mountain slopes munching their way through dinner. Glaciers are up close. The blue hue of the glaciers glows. But those glaciers are visibly shrinking in front of our very eyes. Visitors now see open rock where only recently the glacier filled that space. The glaciers recede and shrivel as the climate changes and the earth warms.

In the preserved nature of a national park, God's creation is right in your face. Agents of the natural world are at work all around and you can see them at work. The year that I visited Glacier National Park, lightning had recently struck the pine forest that was dry from several years of previous drought. That lightning strike sparked a forest fire that had destroyed large swaths of the forest, well beyond the deliberate burns controlled by park rangers to keep the forest healthy. This fire certainly had been out of control. Brittle, charred ashes continued for miles and miles. Blackened sticks stood bare, silhouetted starkly against the skyline of the hillside where once there were stately lush green trees. As I stood amidst this desolation, the crinkle of ash beneath my feet, the seeable horizon filled with charred sticks that once were stately trees. Devastation was palpable. It seemed impossible that life here was a possibility. Is this the desolation toward which earth is headed? How can life find a way? Are we headed toward one big desolate disaster area?

Out of the corner of my eye, I caught a glimpse that has shaped my worldview ever since. I glimpsed green. I turned and bent down. Peeking up through the ash were leaves of a plant that had dug and clawed its way through the destruction to reach the air and reach out to the sky. It was pushing aside the destruction as a sign that life would continue in that place. That life would be different than before. It would take time—oh, so much time. And hopefully no roads would cover it over, or well-meaning tourists would trample it beneath our feet. That green slip of a plant had emerged as new life.

The plant image amidst blackened forest helped sustain me in the work of disaster recovery in which I would later be very involved. In disaster, the starkness of contrasts is right in front of us. The bleakness, the destruction of what was, the mess, the uprootedness. And amidst this, pushing through with the strength that pushes through the despair, are blades of grass; a glimpse of new life; symbol of hope for what may become.

Glacier National Park, Montana, 2008. Photo by author.

Glacier National Park, Montana, 2008. Photo by author.

That sign of green—of new life—has seemed a sign of God's presence. God is there. God is there in the suffering. God is there amidst the destruction. God is hurt by the disaster. But God and God's work of creation is not defined by despair. God is pushing through the rubble, breaking through the ash, springing forth life and healing from the inside, using what is there to create and co-create with natural agents—Life Again! God is sustainer.

Already Resilient

A natural disaster can disrupt people's lives in the most devastating ways. People fear for the order and security of the very space they inhabit. The unexpectedness of a disaster event and the seeming randomness of those impacted compounds that lack of control. The loss of loved ones and treasured personal belongings create holes in people's lives. The once-assumed order of the world shatters.

The journey to wholeness and healing includes assigning meaning to the event and to the experience of recovery. Meaning provides order and a version of control. Theology is important for this process. God-language helps people make meaning of their experiences. It embodies faith and points to strength. It can motivate accompaniment, solidarity, and justice. Other understandings of God can facilitate fatalism and facilitate blame of victims or scapegoating vulnerable groups for tragedies. Therefore, the type of God-talk in which we engage matters. The symbols on which we rely and the God-language we use shape personal and community understandings of God's very nature and of God's actions. The nature of the relationship between God and the world, in turn, shape the way response and recovery happen. It presents a vision of what a society and community look like when recovery is complete and a "new normal" achieved.

This theology in the thin places created by disaster rests on the agency and criteria of people on the margins of society. Remember, disasters create margins and marginalize people. Resilience as part of theology amidst disaster though points to a response that is not based on people's needs or limitations but in their strengths. It is not a needs-based mission, but a *grace-ful mission* based in the very nature and action of God that is strength and beauty.[1] This theology starts with the reality that people and communities already practice resilience, through their very survival. Jon Sobrino talks about the people in El Salvador who experience multiple

---

1. Blaufuss, "Unexpected Agents," 441–51.

disasters and multiple injustices and inequalities and continue to fight for life over and over.[2]

A healing *new normal* does not mean getting back to the *way things were*. That system likely arranged itself inequitably in the first place. Instead, Jesus' *new normal* is a vision that makes the well-being of those who begin as excluded or vulnerable or marginalized the very criteria for the emerging system and order. God's sustaining love that makes this "newness" possible is personal and it is systemic. God's sustaining love expresses beauty beyond imagination and embodies the long-term power of resilience.

Faith Symbols Aid Meaning Making

People make personal meaning through theology and God-talk. I recall specific stories from people in New Orleans during recovery efforts through the United Church of Christ following 2005 Hurricane Katrina. New Orleans is part of the United States' *Bible Belt*. People use God-language openly. They both blame and credit God for events with these phrases. "Bless your heart." "I am blessed." "Why me?" can emerge from the same breath.

Hazel Moore fled her home in New Orleans before it was deluged by the flood after Hurricane Katrina in 2005. Water filled the house like a basin. It sat in her home for weeks. Ms. Hazel lamented that she felt too old to begin life again in that house. She decided to live with her children. But she wanted to see the house one last time. As she walked in the house, she saw furniture destroyed. Papers and clothing lay strewn around the floor as muck. But on the kitchen table, just where she had left it when she evacuated weeks earlier, sat a hymnal. It lay undisturbed. That book contained songs through which she had sung her faith all the years of her life. That hymnal always went with her to church. Its presence on the most used place in the house (that kitchen table) showed how important it was to her. When Ms. Hazel saw that *New Century Hymnal* sitting untouched on the table while surrounded

2. Sobrino, *Where Is God?*

by so much other destruction, she wept. She wept for what she lost. But she wept also for what remained. Her family remained strong. Her faith continued constant.

Collective Meaning Making, National Identity for Bangladesh

Communities also shape their purpose. The whole history of Bangladesh is one of agency as resilience. Bangladesh was created as a nation-state from disaster. The cyclone of 1970 killed three hundred thousand to five hundred thousand people who lived at the mouth of the Ganges River in what was then East Pakistan. The region consists of low-lying marshy lands and islands constantly susceptible to flooding. The slope of the terrain contributes to relatively small increases in sea levels flooding large areas of land. The shape of the Bay of Bengal is conducive to large storm surges. Devastating floods result when those surges come at high tide. "When the waters arrive, there is no place to run."[3] The cyclone of 1970 presented no exception. The storm surge flooded almost a quarter of East Pakistan's landmass. Many people survived by climbing trees, but hundreds of thousands perished. The flood destroyed 65 percent of East Pakistan's fishing industry. Countries such as India and China offered aid, but the East Pakistan central government did not respond. Four months later, in March 1971, East Pakistan declared its independence from the West. This precipitated a ten-month civil war after which East Pakistan gained its independence from the British Empire and the nation-state of Bangladesh emerged. The history of Bangladesh since has centered on its resilience in response to continuing disasters.

> The advent of satellite detection and computer modeling of tropical cyclones, coupled with modern communication systems, coordinated evacuation plans, and the construction of cyclone shelters, offer the hope that the staggering historical death tolls from Ganges delta cyclones may never be repeated. But history teaches us

3. Emanuel, *Divine Wind*, 221.

that a cyclone-free decade or two is all that it takes for a society to forget its past and let down its guard. Where hurricanes are concerned, there is no substitute for constant vigilance.[4]

Foezullah Talukdar, head of the climate change program of the Christian Commission for Development in Bangladesh (CCDP), noted in an October 2020 presentation as part of an Eden Seminary public lecture series, the continuing resilience needed to survive and to thrive in Bangladesh. "They do thrive."[5]

Resilience is the embodiment of God's sustaining love; the faith that life will find a way. For Christians resilience is belief in Jesus' resurrection in which new life triumphs over death. The criteria of what resilience looks like, therefore, is determined by those who are most vulnerable and most negatively impacted by disruptions of disasters. In the same 2020 lecture series in which Foezullah Talukdar shared his experience in Bangladesh, Deenabandhu Manchala, then executive for Southern Asia in Global Ministries (Christian Church Disciples of Christ/United Church of Christ), observed that people are coming together in solidarity and to fight against injustice and abusive powers and for human rights and dignity.

> There seems to be a contagion of resistance against injustice and abuse worldwide. . . . These actions also assert their conviction that what is considered normal should not be the new normal. These are indeed signs of hope to imagine a new world of justice, dignity, and life for all.[6]

Resilience Is Local Knowledge and Action

Resilience is present in local knowledge of the environment. People in Galala Village, Ambon City, Maluku province of Indonesia exemplify this resilience. Yance Zadrak Rumahuru and

---

4. Emanuel, *Divine Wind*, 224.
5. Talukdar, "Implications."
6. Manchala, "Together in Hope."

Augusthina Ch. Kakiay interview people in the area. The geography is prone to disasters including tsunamis, floods, earthquakes, landslides, and volcanoes. The people of Batu Merah tell them that they recognize floods and landslides as cyclical, often linked to the seasons.[7] Another village member describes the signals of disaster. Generally, they look at the clouds. If things are cloudy during the day, but red at night, then there will be heavy rain. However, if the water is dark, there will be no flooding, no matter how heavy the rain.[8] Such responses indicate that the people of Batu Merah have experience to know how to recognize and respond to changes. This local knowledge is reflected in interactions with the Creator and in their congregational worship as well as in actions that protect them from the disruptions or recover when they do create impact.[9]

Resilience also includes knowing what resources already are in your community and using them for well-being, beginning with those most vulnerable and impacted. Neighbors help neighbors. In 2005 New Orleans, in the weeks following Hurricane Katrina, with levee breaks and standing water in the city, the Superdome served as shelter for people made homeless. FEMA set up stations for people to register for assistance. Other people from the community showed up at the Superdome to offer support to fill out the complex forms. Resilience manifests itself as people venture into flooded areas with their own fishing boats to bring their neighbors to dry spaces and safety. Often, people perform these rescues at personal risk. Local resilience manifested itself this way in floods in 2010 Nashville, Tennessee, in 2017 Houston, Texas, and in multiple local communities at many times. Communities of faith regularly offer worship spaces as emergency shelters. Disaster preparedness requires knowing who is in your community as much as it is having a *to-go* bag packed with supplies for an immediate evacuation. Faith leaders who evacuate with church membership lists in hand practice resilience. That information enables leaders

---

7. Rumahuru and Kakiay, "Rethinking Disaster Theology," 630.
8. Rumahuru and Kakiay, "Rethinking Disaster Theology," 630.
9. Rumahuru and Kakiay, "Rethinking Disaster Theology," 631.

to contact the most vulnerable in their community and connect them with safety or resources. Local resilience goes on and on.

Resilience Recognizes Disaster Impact as Situational

Resilience is part of the reality that destruction caused by a disaster can have different impacts on different groups. People who are on the surviving side of the street in the random impact of tornadoes in Moore, Oklahoma, or fires in Southern California experience that disaster differently than those left to rebuild their homes and with their livelihoods destroyed. Survivors' guilt is often a post-traumatic impact of those whose homes and livelihoods are not destroyed by a disaster when their neighbors' are. Care of the community includes those who experience this survivors' guilt.

Resilience offers glimpses of new possibilities. The wide-ranging destruction of the 2004 tsunami in Indonesia, for example, disrupted the long-term war and fighting. As the waves destroyed infrastructure and regrettably lives, they also disrupted power structures and patterns of violence that heretofore seemed unstoppable. John Campbell-Nelson, then my Global Ministries (Christian Church Disciples of Christ/United Church of Christ) mission co-worker in Indonesia, observed a pause in local fighting as impacted people turned their attention from militarism to rebuilding homes and communities. He references Mic 4:3 to name this reality as turning spears into plowshares. "They shall beat their swords into plowshares and their spears into pruning hooks."[10] Even if that pause was temporary and Christians and Muslims went back to naming disaster destruction as divine punishment for the other, possibilities for peace persist.[11]

Situational disaster experience, of course, does not begin in the twenty-first century. Reaching back to another war, in 1274, the Japanese word *kamikaze* emerged to indicate a "divine wind sent by

---

10. Campbell-Nelson, "Religion and Disaster." John and Karen Campbell-Nelson served as mission co-workers with Global Ministries (Christian Church Disciples of Christ/United Church of Christ).

11. Adeney-Risakotta, "Is There a Meaning."

the gods to deliver their land from invaders."[12] War raged between the Mongol commander, Kublai Khan, and the Japanese. Just as the Japanese expected a defeat, a typhoon in the Hakata Bay off Japan's coast devastated the fleet of ships poised to defeat them. The typhoon disrupted the flow of the war. When the Mongols returned to Japan's shores seven years later with an even larger fleet another typhoon devastated that fleet too. The experience cemented into Japanese religiosity that typhoons are *kamikaze, divine wind*. Popular myths in Japan at the time credited the god Raijin with turning the storms against the Mongols. The defeated Mongols, of course, did not see the typhoons as divine intervention, but as the wrath of nature. In Japan, these typhoon-influenced military victories of the late 1200s became the topic of multiple artistic renderings during the 1800s. As Japan ended a long period of national isolation in 1868 following the Meiji Restoration, these disaster-impacted victories reinforced their identity as a nation with divine protection.[13]

---

12. Emanuel, *Divine Wind*, 5.

13. Japanese art featured typhoons and waves beyond the military implications of their influence, such as in the famous wood print *The Great Wave Off Kanagawa* by 1830s Japanese artist Katsushika Hokusai, showcasing Mount Fuji in the background. The people in the painting are miniatures, dots set on the white-cuffed water of the tsunami wave. This wood print was part of a series by Hokusai portraying Mount Fuji. Perhaps the popularity of the print in Japan reflected people's experience during societal upheaval. As Japan's borders opened to those outside Japan, people in the West also took interest in *The Great Wave*. This wood print is one of the most reproduced renderings. By the twenty-first century, the image was common on T-shirts, mugs, and refrigerator magnets, as well as a subject of frequent internet searches. The upheavals of postmodern society also might well be represented in this portrayal of chaos and order in *The Great Wave*.

The Great Wave Off Kanagawa (1830), wood print by Katsushika Hokusai

Resilience Is Innovative

Leaders, both those with positional authority and those with the authority of example, practice resilience as they make decisions that enable whole communities to thrive again. Those decisions might mean trying things not currently in view. Through the years, I have watched up close the positive results of such innovative decisions in the service of community resilience.

Trying New Methods, Valmeyer, Illinois

Long before I was involved professionally with disaster recovery, I watched my home county in southern Illinois experience a devastating flood and recover. In August 1993, floods submerged the region around my hometown of Waterloo in southern Illinois. Waterloo itself sits on high ground in the county and became an evacuation area. The nearby town of Valmeyer, however, sat on the Mississippi River's flood plain. Since its incorporation in 1909, Valmeyer had experienced frequent flooding and cleanup. Primarily a farming community, fields (when not flooded) are fertile. But 1993 was catastrophic for the community. Two waves of flooding came. Levees broke. Waters completely washed away homes, businesses, and livelihoods.

The displaced community seemed poised for permanent scattering. Dennis Knobloch, then mayor of Valmeyer, and other local leaders, considered a proposal by FEMA representatives for Valmeyer to engage in a "planned relocation," otherwise known by FEMA as a "managed retreat." FEMA recently established this hazard mitigation program to move buildings out of the path of recurring disasters. The government offered to buy out damaged properties and let residents use the proceeds to rebuild on higher ground. The Valmeyer project implemented this approach at scale, relocating an entire town. A local farmer agreed to sell his property to the town for a new location on the bluff out of the reach of future flooding.[14] Community leaders realized this might be the only way to keep the community together.[15]

Dr. Nicholas Pinter, a geology professor and flood mitigation expert at the University of California, Davis, observes, "They are really a textbook example of how a town can recover, start over, and thrive after devastation." Pinter credits Valmeyer's successful outcome to its ability to act quickly in the aftermath of the flood as well as a strong and persuasive leadership. "Officials gave people looking for a way to get into a permanent home a viable option as quickly as possible and managed to not have them run away," he says. "They also built broad public support for the effort and ensured that the community had a voice in decisions all throughout the process."[16]

The churches were central to the community's decision to relocate. Pastors were trusted leaders. Community leaders were members of these churches. Then-mayor Dennis Knobloch observes it was difficult to keep social networks alive. They were able to do this because the community's institutions such as the school,

---

14. Hellman, "City Upon a Hill." See also Elam, "Flood Forced This Town."
15. Rossi, "Illinois Town."
16. Rossi, "Illinois Town," para. 28.

churches, and civic groups kept operating despite not having permanent structures.[17] The local Catholic Church, St. Mary, met at Gibault High School located eight miles away in Waterloo for over two years and through a fire at the high school that destroyed a lot of St. Mary's belongings.[18] The United Church of Christ and St. Mary Catholic Church deliberately decided to build next to each other in New Valmeyer so they could share programming and fellowship. St. John UCC's website claims that in 2024, "having come together to rebuild Valmeyer on the bluff after the flood, the parishes now come together for a Fall Church Picnic."[19]

Pinter concludes that rebuilding Valmeyer was a notable feat, but it does not necessarily represent a road map for the future. Today, amid growing climate pressure, it is virtually impossible to carry out such an operation. With unprecedented rates of climate-induced disaster and dwindling governmental funds, most professionals no longer consider rebuilding communities a viable form of disaster recovery."[20] *Science Advances* revealed in 2019 that of the more than forty-three thousand properties FEMA has paid to demolish and return to nature, most of them are in already wealthy counties.[21] The Natural Resources Defense Council (NRDC), reviewing thirty years of FEMA data, found it takes a median of more than five years between a flood and the completion of a FEMA-funded buyout project. The study concludes that "long wait times make buyouts less accessible, less equitable, and less effective for disaster mitigation and climate adaptation."[22] Still, New Valmeyer stands as a testament that the program worked in this location.

17. Rossi, "Illinois Town."
18. St. Mary Catholic Church, "History."
19. St. John United Church of Christ (Valmeyer, IL), https://stjohnvalmeyer.wordpress.com/.
20. Hellman, "City Upon a Hill."
21. Mach et al., "Managed Retreat."
22. Weber and Moor, "Going Under," 4.

Leading by Example, New Orleans, Louisiana—"Recovery Is a Marathon, Not a Sprint"

When everything is in chaos, symbols may be the only way to see through to wholeness. Symbols can actualize a new reality as we see through them to experience newness. For Dale and Jim Bonds in New Orleans a wedding dress symbolized a hope that moved the family through the destruction to recovery for the entire neighborhood. Dale told the story often. In August 2005, the Bonds eagerly anticipated their daughter's upcoming wedding. The dress, chosen with care, lay on the bed to avoid wrinkles. Perhaps the display also encouraged anyone who walked by the room to admire its elegance and beauty. The dress represented hope for a new life together about to begin for this couple. It soon came to play a different symbolic role. On the day of evacuation before Hurricane Katrina no one in the family thought about that wedding dress. They left for safety. The waters came. Weeks later, they returned. Flood waters had crumbled the foundations of the home. Receding waters left soaked belongings strewn around the house. And yet when the family returned, they found that dress still lying on the bed, untouched.

Dale and Jim Bonds gutted the inside of their house but did nothing else with the house for some time. They tried to decide whether to rebuild or to move as they started over. Finally, they decided to rebuild in the same location. That decision was a leap of faith. Dale and Jim had resources to rebuild, but the neighborhood around them was gone. No grocery stores or businesses in the community had yet come back. No other homeowners around the neighborhood yet had begun rebuilding. Dale and Jim finally decided to be the first, to anchor the community. Perhaps it was the new life they saw through the symbolism of that wedding dress that enabled them to hope and plan for new life. They imagined what life could be and made it what it is while encouraging and inspiring others. Eventually, other homeowners rebuilt and schools, businesses, and grocery stores returned. The neighborhood now thrives.[23]

Resilience as Partnership

Resilience embodies a partnership among those outside the disaster's impact and those who survive. Eleazar Fernandez, Filipino-American Christian theologian, roots a partnership relation in the image of God. A theology of partnership, Fernandez contends, is intrinsic relatedness within the web of life.[24] "Relationship is our fundamental reality. In the beginning is relationship. Relationship is constitutive of who we are and of what we can become. Relationship, not rationality, is decisive for our humanity."[25] Fernandez references Desmond Tutu's *Ubuntu* theology, rooted in Xhosa expression (Tutu's people) *Ubuntu ungamntu ngabanye abantu*. It communicates that each individual's humanity is ideally expressed in relationship with others. He references George Tinker's description of the Native American Lakota phrase *mitakouye oyasin* for "all my relations" that articulates the intrinsic relationship of all creatures. It intends that the well-being of the ecosystem is our well-being not because we make use of the ecosystem but because our very being is intrinsically one with the ecosystem.[26] From this starting point of relationship, then, Fernandez asserts: "Then it is also what makes us truly an image of God. Relationship is the primary lens through which we interpret the notion of the image of God."[27]

This emphasis on relationship and the image of God then guides the interactions that we have with one another, including in response to disaster and resilience. Fernandez calls us to beware of *outreach* in the guise of church partnerships. He notes the efforts

---

23. Klinenberg illustrates how anchor institutions and leaders help communities recover. Klinenberg, *Palaces for the People*.
24. Fernandez, "Theology of Partnership."
25. Fernandez, "Theology of Partnership," 26.
26. Tinker, "American Indian," 158.
27. Fernandez, "Theology of Partnership," 27.

of churches to move away from old and disempowering ways of doing global mission/ministries; toward autonomy and self-reliance, capacity-building programs for missionized churches, inculturation projects, partnership as critical presence and mission in reverse. But he warns that we need to constantly be vigilant and critical of practices that continue to perpetuate asymmetrical relations.[28]

Joerg Rieger, in "Theology and Mission Between Colonialism and Postcolonialism," is even more pointed in the relationships involved in who makes decisions. When the question of the one with power is "What can we do?" it indicates a position of power and privilege. Rieger says instead the right question is "How might we be part of the problem?"[29] I agree that mission as outreach may be valid in response to immediate needs. However, when it focuses on the goodness and generosity of the sender at the expense of concealing the asymmetrical power relations, it needs to be challenged.

Presence as Partnership, Sri Lanka

The horror of the 2004 tsunami in southern Asia/western Africa was unimaginable. The day began with no problems. The sun shone. Survivors regularly reflect that the only thing out of the ordinary they noticed were the actions of the animals of land and sea. Suddenly, the beach lay bare where usually the waters covered the land. We know the earthquake that caused the tsunami sucked the waters into the crack in the earth. And then the terrible crash of tsunami waves plucked people from their daily lives. Some people survived while others washed out to sea with the recoil of the wave. The randomness of losses seems unbearable. The randomness of survivors is equally as inexplainable. Diane Fonderlin, who served as a Global Ministries (Christian Church Disciples of Christ/United Church of Christ) volunteer in the southern

---

28. Fernandez, "Theology of Partnership," 25–26.
29. Rieger, "Theology and Mission," 201–27.

Asia region soon after the tsunami, regularly tells of the story she heard of a little girl's survival. A man caught hold of a tree during the wave. Simultaneously, he reached out and grabbed the girl, still able to hang on. Both man and little girl survived. The story shaped Diane's understanding of her own role in the disaster recovery. It symbolizes the power of presence. The man happened to be in the right place at the right time. Global systems for response and recovery, of which Diane was part, could also be present even if not planned. God intends life. People can be God's arms in the embodiment of that vision.

Random Resilience and Interconnected Complexity

Just as creation is complex and multilayered, often presenting as random and chaotic, people can also experience resilience as random. That randomness emerges from the interconnected relationships of reality. Resilience is layers of a complex causal weave in which people strengthen each other rather than tearing each other down. Partnership as resilience that is complex interconnection abounds in Christian Scripture. One person's well-being is tied up with the well-being of all. The prophet Jeremiah in Scripture communicated the shape of the society that was to form as people came back from exile: "For in its [the city of exile's] welfare you will find your welfare" (Jer 29:7). When the United Church of Christ formed a national Disaster Ministries office, leaders chose Gal 6:2 to guide the work, "Bear one another's burdens." Later, Deenabandhu Manchala, former Global Ministries' southern Asia area executive, highlights partnership as the interconnectedness of the world in the relationships through which the good news of God's reign comes alive.[30] As such, partnership for justice and life is not only the means towards an end but also the result itself. Manchala called it the eschatological fulfillment of God's grand plan of salvation through reconciliation "to be put into effect when the times reach their fulfillment—to bring unity to all things in heaven and

---

30. Manchala, "Together in Hope."

on earth under Christ." Based on Eph 1:10 "as a plan for the fullness of time, to gather up all things in him, things in heaven and things on earth." This interconnectedness leads to outcomes that are random, unexplainable, and unimaginably beautiful.

New Normal

The terminology of *new normal* used often in times of disaster to indicate the need to adapt to the disruption can be used to reinforce power relationships that made particular people or groups more vulnerable to greater impact in the first place. Instead, religious communities in natural disaster mitigation and recovery are important because with our resources of faith and tradition we bring a lens that *new normal* does not just mean put things back the way they were. So, we work with others to build hurricane resistant homes. *New normal* does not mean accepting that the disaster created a "clean slate" where an outsider with access to resources can plan the community back in the way that outsider envisions (to their advantage). Instead, that faith lens necessitates relationship-building and listening and advocating so that rebuilding is about local decisions; and then within those local realities, to hold space for the preference of those usually without power. In this, what the world calls *new* really is brought closer to the way God originally intends and the way Jesus is bringing into being always.

So "new normal" terminology could be helpful. It helps with making meaning of the disaster. It helps with creating continuity and stability, and something to count on, amidst our brokenness. But the faith perspective we can bring to what emerges is a normal that does not reinforce power inequities or ways that destroy again. Instead, it is a normal in the way that Jesus makes all things new. Jesus' normal is this: "The greatest among you will be your servant. All who exalt themselves will be humbled, and all who humble themselves will be exalted" (Matt 23:11–12).

Resilience therefore involves collaboration and figuring it out together. It prioritizes the voices and the decisions of those most often excluded. It makes the warp and weave of relationship mutual. Partnerships that find a way forward in the complexity will strengthen the ties that bind. If creation is complex, open-ended, communal; and redemption is collaborative; then sustenance is the resilience of the most vulnerable who exercise agency in making decisions. These actions will bring together those layers and strands in ways that build up that world and will bring those strands into relationship with each other in ways that uphold.

Chapter 8

God's Sustaining Love

> "And remember, I am with you always, to the end of the age." Matthew 28:20b

THEOLOGIES EMERGE FROM THE thin places of disaster to reflect and address the complexity of the situation in that time. Theologies in thin places also affirm the presence and action of God over time. God's sustaining love is for the long term. Disaster recovery that builds resilient communities also is long-term and sustaining. For Christians, the last verses of Matthew can offer inspiration. The final phrases of Matt 28:18–20 are a window into the nature of God and God's sustaining love that creates and supports resilient community. Theologies in thin places emerge from and join God in this long-term, complex, and sustaining love.

> And Jesus came and said to them, "All authority in heaven and on earth has been given to me. Go therefore and make disciples of all nations, baptizing them in the name of the Father and of the Son and of the Holy Spirit, and teaching them to obey everything that I have commanded you. And remember, I am with you always, to the end of the age."

This passage, often named *the Great Commission* by its readers, has been examined and parsed for mission theologies that emphasize completely different approaches and look to different outcomes. Mission as outward movement emerges from the sending directive of "go." Activities for Jesus-following emerge from the "make disciples" phrase. The multiple places of mission and mission as community impact explore the meaning of "nations," especially as the contemporary nation-state had not yet been invented at the time of this writing and first English translations. A mission focus on baptism and incorporation into a community of faith roots itself in this passage. Theologies of who God is as Trinity emphasize the trifold formula for naming God as expressed in these verses. Questions of human identity formation, naming, and relationships have been influenced by this self-naming act of God. Mission as a deeper dive into the content of beliefs and mission to influence and shape society have emphasized the "teaching them to obey everything that I have commanded you" content of this passage.

For all its emphasis on human response and activities, however, the frame for the "Great Commission" is affirmation of who God is and the nature of God's action. The passage is a postresurrection appearance of Jesus to the disciples. As I have highlighted in previous chapters, theological method incorporates authenticity, authority, and accountability. This passage incorporates all those parts. Jesus' authenticity, authority, and accountability here are the reality of his crucifixion and resurrection and the implications for all creation. Authenticity: Jesus as God's Son was willing to be killed to live the full reality of the good news of God's abundance for all that he proclaimed. Authority: Even death could not keep the good news from coming into reality in the world. Resurrection is the authority of God's new life. And accountability.

This passage practices accountability that is Jesus' resurrection in the complexity of community that is both ordered and chaotic. The disciples are living the reality of new life in Jesus' resurrection-presence, but that community is not whole. The disciples still live in the brokenness and disruption of the crucifixion. The passage names eleven as the remaining number of disciples. Judas is no longer among them, and Matthias has not yet been added to their number (Acts 1). The community of accountability is situated in a particular geographic place that is both stable and disordered. The meeting takes place on mountain in Galilee to which Jesus has directed them. The lack of specific directions for how to get there indicates a familiarity with the mountain in their home region of Galilee. Familiar space indicates stability. Yet, what they have come to expect of that place is thoroughly disrupted by what they experience there with the resurrected Jesus. When those eleven see the risen Jesus, they have mixed and extreme reactions. Some worship and some doubt. People impacted by natural disasters experience similar conflicting reactions. Stability is disrupted, even the stability of sorrow and loss in knowing that death is death. The life amidst expected death throws the situation into chaos.

This mix of stable and chaotic space for accountability sets the scene for those disciples to experience the nature and action of God. Jesus claims his authority. As a postresurrection appearance, Jesus' authority is life that contests death and destruction. That authority is cosmic, "all authority in heaven and on earth" (Matt 28:18). The authority emerges from the communal actions of the divine, "has been given to me" by God (v. 18). And the resurrected Jesus uses that authority to give the disciples instructions for authentic actions: go, make disciples, baptize, name, teach, obey Jesus' commands. By the second part of v. 20 (and the ending to the canonical version of Matthew's Gospel), all those pieces of authenticity, authority, and accountability, both for the resurrected Jesus, and for the human community, are rolled together in an interactive whole. "And remember, I am with you always, to the end of the age." God's sustaining love that overcomes even death and destruction for the purpose of abundant life is ever present. The passage that begins with the particularity of a certain place and time on a Galilean mountain extends into the expansiveness of time, "to the end of the age." God's sustaining love makes community resilience possible.

Long-Term and Cumulative Disasters

Community resilience is necessary for surviving and thriving. In the first two decades of the twenty-first century, natural disasters have been documented as more frequent and more intense than previously recorded.[1] In addition, the nature of natural disasters often is not a single event, but the accumulation of slow onset and long-lasting environmental situations such as drought. Climate change certainly creates disasters.

These more frequent, intense events and longer lasting disaster situations impact the resilience of communities and make that resilience more necessary. Disaster response organizations previously have worked sequentially. They try to mitigate the devastation of natural disasters by helping people prepare to evacuate temporarily. After an event the organizations can focus on recovery and rebuilding to help people return home to put their lives back together on stable ground. Today, preparation and mitigation are still important. Resilient communities need to know their neighbors, plan for emergencies, and be aware of how to access wider resources for assistance in recovery and rebuilding. In more frequent and intense disaster situations, however, the same communities often experience new disaster situations while still in the process of recovering from previous destruction. In long-term disaster situations, resilient communities also need the power to survive during the prolonged period itself. Recovery actions are concurrent rather than sequential. In this reality of frequent and long-term disaster situations, the fields of humanitarian assistance and community development intertwine. And faith communities, in Christian circles with characteristics of *koinonia*, *diakonia*, and justice, emerge as important actors.

---

1. EM-DAT: The International Disaster Database, https://emdat.be/.

Long-Term Accompaniment Is Community Resilience

Faith Communities Bring Accountability to the Process

Disaster risk reduction (DRR) goals are broader than response and recovery to singular events. These goals embody a commitment to wholeness and well-being over time, looking to root causes of disasters and encouraging actions toward disaster risk reduction. It is a collective process. Local communities connected to larger organizations have access to technical expertise in rebuilding and recovery from other local communities that have experienced and developed skills and methods in their own places. Technical skills in disaster mitigation and response and risk reduction are available to organizations that bring government and nongovernmental resources together for this work. These organizations have broad scope and reach to incorporate these values into actions that have wider scale than any community alone. At the same time, local faith communities influence the very approach and values of these larger organizations. Values of accompaniment, resilience, well-being, and abundance emerge from faith communities and influence the larger practice of disaster recovery and are utilized and implemented at large scale.

Global organizations have recognized the need to concentrate on disaster risk reduction to support resilient communities. The United Nations Office for Disaster Risk Reduction (UNDRR) embodies this recognition and informs approaches. The framework adopted in Sendai, Japan, in 2015 at the third UN World Conference for DRR sets goals for achievement by 2030. These goals aim for community resilience with the following vision.

> The ability of a system, community or society exposed to hazards to resist, absorb, accommodate, adapt to, transform and recover from the effects of a hazard in a timely and efficient manner, including through the preservation and restoration of its essential basic structures and functions through risk management.[2]

2. United Nations Office for Disaster Risk Reduction, "Resilience."

Disaster response organizations that use community resilience as a guide and outcome for their work value local knowledge, community networks and relationships, communication, health, governance and leadership, resources, economic investment, preparedness, and mental outlook.[3] Brian Mayer's review of scholarly literature in 2019 identifies community disaster resilience as attention to, and investment in, local capacities for adaptation to a changing and uncertain environment. It recognizes the mechanism of social capital to reduce disaster impact and enhance recovery. Communities' adaptive capacities are primary.[4]

National and international organizations working on disaster risk reduction focus on aspects of community that demonstrate and further equip their resilience. These outside organizations can facilitate factual knowledge, collective efficacy and empowerment, training, and education by coming alongside local knowledge that mitigates vulnerabilities through how it understands the risks of the community. They emphasize that community networks and relationships embody connectedness and cohesion, helping people deal with uncertainty after a disaster.

Effective communication, whether risk or crisis communication, helps a community to articulate, coordinate, and understand the risk and impact of disasters. During a crisis local and frontline leadership needs clear roles and engagement. Current literature in DRR highlights governance as an important response tool. This research emphasizes fair distribution of resources to help communities in the short term, while economic investment is a longer term intervention to promote resilience. Lastly, mental outlook arguably has the most potential to build resilience within a community through a focus on subelements such as hope and adaptability.[5]

Communities of faith can play diverse roles in these aspects of community resilience depending on the theology that shapes that community. The shape of that theology held by individuals, those understandings of the nature of God, matter. Secular and

3. Patel et al., "What Do We Mean."
4. Mayer, "Review of the Literature."
5. Patel et al., "What Do We Mean."

civil society disaster response mechanisms in the United States and globally regularly include "emotional and spiritual care" as integral to the response, recovery and rebuilding process.[6] The resource *Light Our Way* by the National VOAD is one example of the emphasis on spiritual care in times of disaster.

Light Our Way: A Guide for Spiritual Care in Times of Disaster, 2018
National Voluntary Organizations Active in Disaster (NVOAD)

Christian pastoral counseling takes seriously people's perceptions of God in processing their trauma and suffering. Storm Swain explores God concepts present in disaster spiritual care during response to the attacks on the World Trade Center in New

---

6. Examples: NVOAD, ACT Alliance, United Nations. See also National Voluntary Organizations Active in Disaster, *Light Our Way*.

York City on September 11, 2001. She worked among chaplains at the 9/11 Temporary Mortuary (T. Mort.) following the attacks. Swain begins her book, *Trauma and Transformation at Ground Zero*, observing, "Undertaking any endeavor where one seeks to be true to the profound task of holding the stories of those who have worked at the face of trauma, and the story of God within that, is a humbling task."[7] Through engagement with these responders as theologians, Swain offers a model of pastoral care as "earth-making, pain-bearing, life-giving."[8] That pastoral care model addresses emotional and spiritual care in the midst of natural disasters as well.

The same is true of collective communities of faith as with individuals. Communities also can lean into blame and close themselves off from participation by all members. It is possible that communities have experienced so much oppression that the focus is only short-term survival and not long-term vision. This mental outlook that builds resilience though is closely tied to the meaning and purpose and connections that also can be part of communities of faith. That hope and adaptability needed for community resilience can be rooted in the theology embraced by persons within those communities of faith. Theology matters.

Resilience in a Prolonged Disaster

This role of theology is important in the long-term recovery from a single disaster event. It is even more vital as multiple sequential or simultaneous disaster situations wreak havoc on a community or when disasters events themselves are prolonged. Resilience amidst a disaster that is not an event, but an ongoing trauma, is not only response and rebuilding, but necessitates constant commitment and connection with each other.

---

7. Swain, *Trauma and Transformation*, vii.
8. Swain, *Trauma and Transformation*, 182.

Climate Refugees: Permanent Temporariness in Global Migration

The frequency and intensity of disaster situations and the prolonged impact of long-term climate change creates a constant state of upheaval and destruction that displaces people permanently from their homes. Disasters create internally displaced persons within their countries and disasters create refugees forced to flee across national boundaries. For example, Hurricane Irene caused so much upheaval in Puerto Rico in 2017, that the movement of people to the mainland accelerated. Disaster response of the United Church of Christ, among others, focused on support of displaced families and movement to the mainland as much as on repair of homes on the island.

Climate refugees are so widespread that the United States immigration system identifies disaster displaced people within its immigration policies. Global migration resulting from climate change is exploding. Almost every refugee crisis has a climate change component. Drought is a major source of hunger and a precipitator of violence from which families are fleeing the Northern Triangle of Central America (Honduras, Guatemala, El Salvador). Political tensions in Syria in 2016 were exacerbated by water shortages caused by climate change, resulting in widespread displacement both inside and outside the country. Drought and water shortages around the Great Lakes in eastern Africa have displaced people from Burundi, the Democratic Republic of the Congo, Ethiopia, Kenya, Malawi, Rwanda, Tanzania, Uganda, and more. Community resilience in face of this *permanent temporariness* seems impossible. *New York Times* journalist Abrahm Lustgarten observes the slingshot effects of drought and floods exacerbated by climate change. "As their land fails them, hundreds of millions of people from Central America to Sudan to the Mekong Delta will be forced to choose between flight or death. The result will almost certainly be the greatest wave of global migration the world has seen."[9] Lustgarten advocates planning. "The only way to mitigate

---

9. Lustgarten, "Great Climate Migration," para. 4.

the most destabilizing aspects of mass migration is to prepare for it, and preparation demands a sharper imagining of where people are likely to go, and when."[10]

This planning can be informed by a theological vision of interconnectedness, in which what impacts one impacts all. That interconnectedness takes on greater urgency. The well-being envisioned in the beauty of creation requires more than effective cooperation and accompaniment. This community resilience requires adaptation, advocacy, and community organizing.

Adaptation, Advocacy, and Community Organizing

Joseph and Family in Genesis 45

The theological vision for this long-term and sustained action is present throughout Christian Scripture. The story of Joseph and his brothers in Egypt as told in Gen 45:3–11, 15 recognizes precedent for adaptation amid long-term and sequential disaster situations. The story of Joseph weaves its way through the book of Genesis. In the encounter of this passage, Joseph's brothers, impacted by drought, have come to Egypt seeking food for the family's survival. "In a single artistic moment," writes Old Testament scholar and theologian, Walter Brueggemann, "the entire plot is made visible."[11] Brueggemann notes the buildup of tension in the latter chapters of Genesis between God and empire, embodied here as the tension between the family of Israel and Egypt. By chapter 45 Joseph had been double crossed and abandoned by his brothers, served time in jail, and interpreted dreams. As the story's plot twists and turns, Joseph now serves as a high official in the Egyptian government and the family is threatened by drought. The brothers approach Egypt seeking relief from the famine gripping the outlying areas. They encounter a high-ranking official,

---

10. Lustgarten, "Great Climate Migration," para. 16.
11. Brueggemann, *Genesis*, 343.

not imagining it might be their brother. "In this scene, the plot is larger than every player, including Joseph."[12]

Joseph recognizes his brothers and finally identifies himself to them. Joseph's self-disclosure in verse three of this forty-fifth chapter is dramatic. Simply, "I am Joseph" (Gen 45:3). Yet, it is so much more. The grammar demonstrates a position of power and influence in the empire. He chooses the time and place for this self-disclosure. Joseph is proclaiming, not asking. Yet, the content of the name by which he identifies himself self-consciously places him amidst the people. Joseph is his family name, not the name of the empire. In this very announcement, Joseph identifies that he can influence systems and that he will do so from the perspective of the people.

A 2019 webinar on "Climate Change and Forced Global Migration," sponsored by the United Church of Christ Environmental Justice Office, opened with reflections by Rev. Michael Malcom, executive director, Alabama Interfaith Power and Light. He observed that both this story and our relationship with the planet moves from mitigation into adaptation. In mitigation, action focuses on prevention and lessening the negative effects of, in this case, disruption, disaster, and drought. Adaptation, however, acknowledges that the catastrophic change is already upon us and the action of agency is to adapt.[13]

I agree and contend that the agency in adaptation also emboldens resilience. The brothers in Gen 45 act to save the family. They are doing what is necessary to adapt to the changing landscape. They also are developing a new relationship of resilience with that landscape. When the brothers and Joseph meet again after all those years, Joseph is in a position of influence to actively redistribute resources. By identifying with the family in that statement of self-disclosure, Joseph commits himself to using his influence to put the storehouses of Egypt at the service of the people's survival. The resources of empire, at this moment, would be harnessed to create life and not continue to death.

12. Brueggemann, *Genesis*, 343.
13. Midgett-Crosby, "Creation Justice Webinar."

Global forced migration is a reality throughout the world. People are forcibly displaced by war, violence, discrimination, poverty, climate change, and climate catastrophes. Populations are shifting. Climate change creates changes to which cultures and populations cannot adapt fast enough to encounter as life-giving. Disaster, conflict, and famine result. People are resilient and the earth has resources, but their distribution is not matched equitably.

Joseph's commitment to using the resources of empire for the benefit of the people is the beginning of this passage. The relationship and opportunity to figure out together how to do this, ends the passage Gen 45:15, "He kissed all his brothers and wept upon them, and after that his brothers talked with him."

Resisting Climate Change

Likewise, youth in the United States acting for climate justice received a global platform when the United Church of Christ sponsored Kiran Oommen to make a presentation at the November 2018 World Children's Day conference of the World Council of Church and UNICEF.[14] Oommen shared reflections on *Juliana v. U.S.*, in which twenty-one youth, including him, filed a lawsuit against the United States government for its role in causing climate change and violating their rights to life, liberty, and property, while also failing to protect essential public resources. The United Church of Christ called for sermons in support of this action. Justice for #EachGeneration.[15]

Caterina Tino, Communications Specialist for UNICEF, thanks Kiran for his commitment and action. "What you and the other young plaintiffs are doing is remarkable and a source of inspiration for many (regardless of how it will end)." Tino positively recognizes the link with churches in this action.

> Churches have the power to take an initiative by an individual or a small group of people and give it a platform

---

14. Tino, "WCC's Engagement for Children."
15. United Church of Christ, "Justice for #EachGeneration."

to reach a much bigger community of people. They are amplifiers and epicenters of social change movements, and we do need them on board if we want to advance the child rights agenda. I am grateful the UCC is already a champion on this front, and I look forward to continued collaboration in the future.[16]

These actions led the way for a 2023 case making its way through the United States court system in which youth sued the state of Montana with the coordination of the organization Our Children's Trust. With the Held v. Montana ruling a district court affirmed that climate is included in the state constitution's guarantee of a right to a "clean and healthful environments." It struck down a provision in the Montana Environmental Policy Act that barred the state from considering climate impacts when permitting energy projects.[17]

Joseph's self-disclosure in Gen 45, "I am Joseph," signals his commitment to using his influence for the purpose of life-giving action. His embrace of his brothers jump-starts the conversation that shapes that action. Our commitments and actions matter in the same way as Joseph and his brothers. Addressing global forced migration and advocating for climate justice make us part of the adaptation and resilience needed to embody God's dream of abundance for all.

Tuvalu in South Pacific, Canary in the Coal Mine

As we come to the end of this book, the people of the South Pacific nation of Tuvalu greet us. They live in the thin places of imminent and long-term catastrophic disaster. Rising sea levels caused by rapid climate change are literally causing the nation of Tuvalu to disappear. Sea water is covering the islands of Tuvalu at a rate that will soon submerge all habitable land. Rev. James Bhagwan, general secretary of the Pacific Conference of Churches in 2019, estimates that climate induced relocation will be necessary by 2029.

16. Tino, "WCC's Engagement for Children."
17. Selig, "Youths Sued Montana."

"We are talking about climate-induced displacements in countries that will literally be submerged by the ocean. People are relocating because their land is disappearing. And our brothers and sisters are facing extreme weather patterns, and the slow suffering of drought."[18] Tuvalu leaders name their situation as a canary in the coal mine for the rest of the world.

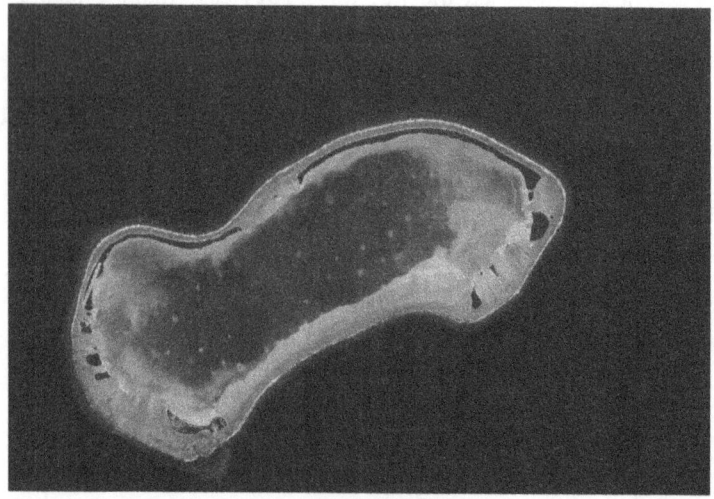

Tuvalu nation in South Pacific Ocean, 2024

This loss is material and it is spiritual. The people of Tuvalu practice a spirituality that is tied intimately with the particular land of their island home. "It's an intrinsic relationship that includes Christian spirituality and cultural spirituality," says Rev. Bhagwan. When a child is born, grandparents or parents bury the umbilical cord under a tree. As that tree grows and we grow, it is a reminder that the person is part of the land.[19] People's culture, ancestors, and identity are all tied to that land. They know intimately God's continuing creation. Loss of land is a loss of culture and identity. Bhagwan calls disaster a "spiritual trauma."

People of Tuvalu practice accompaniment and solidarity in the face of current and pending disaster.

18. Bhagwan, "Climate-Induced Displacement," para. 7.
19. Bhagwan, "Climate-Induced Displacement," para. 9.

In practical terms, the resilience of Pasifika communities is grounded in faith and trust in God and strengthened by reengaging and reclaiming the traditional wisdom of our elders in their ability to relate, read the weather patterns and live in a respectful and mutual relationship with the environment while embracing new technologies such as mapping and warning systems.[20]

Leaders link care for creation with discipleship. In a series of Bible studies in 2018, Rev. Geraldine Williams, Rev. Koloma Makewin, and Rev. Dr. Seforosa Carroll explore Ps 104, Matt 7:24–27, Luke 14:15–24, and the book of Job. The study's core statement claims that custodianship of creation is integral to active discipleship. Churches and Christians have the responsibility to be prepared to respond to and mitigate the impact of disasters.[21]

This accompaniment and solidarity seeking justice strengthens the community resilience already active. Disaster theology of the South Pacific is not passive theology but a proclamation of resilience. In meetings facilitated by the Uniting Church in Australia, leaders in the Pacific Conference of Churches emphasized that faith and trust in God's unwavering love is expressed through Christian discipleship, resilience, love, and hope. They affirmed that resilience enables individuals and communities to build "communities of sustainability in the face of disaster."[22] These leaders conclude, "A theology of disaster resilience acknowledges that there are no easy answers to the problem of suffering. However, a theology of disaster resilience rests on the conviction and trust that God through Christ is present in the Spirit amidst disasters, suffering and despair."[23]

The call to discipleship by leaders of the Pacific Conference of Churches brings us full circle in this exploration of theology

---

20. Uili et al., "Theology of Disaster Resilience," 1–2.

21. Uili et al., "Theology of Disaster Resilience."

22. Carroll and Theology of Disaster Working Group, "Theology of Disaster Resilience," 3.

23. Carroll and Theology of Disaster Working Group, "Theology of Disaster Resilience," 2.

in thin places. God's sustaining presence is an active love amidst suffering and despair. The resurrected Jesus' claim "I will be with you to the end of the age" is embodied in the preparedness, the mitigation, the long-term commitment to adaptation, advocacy against climate change, and community organizing for disaster resilience. Communities of faith embody these commitments and shape networks beyond themselves to implement God's vision of abundance and well-being for all.

Friends in Tuvalu, we stand with you in the thin places of disaster. You practice a powerful example of accompaniment, solidarity, and resilience. We join you. May the whole world know God's sustaining love that is with us until the end of the age creating beauty and abundance more than we can imagine.

Bibliography

Adeney-Risakotta, Bernard. "Is There a Meaning in Natural Disaster? Constructions of Culture, Religion, and Science." *Exchange: Journal of Contemporary Christianities in Context* 38 (January 2009) 226–43.

Antal, James. *Climate Church, Climate World: How People of Faith Must Work for Change*. Rev. ed. Lanham, MD: Rowman & Littlefield, 2023.

Aten, Jamie. *A Walking Disaster: What Surviving Katrina and Cancer Taught Me About Faith and Resilience*. West Conshohocken, PA: Templeton Press, 2018.

Bhagwan, James. "Climate-Induced Displacement Is Traumatizing Generations of People." Interview with World Council of Churches, December 12, 2019. https://www.oikoumene.org/news/rev-james-bhagwan-climate-induced-displacement-is-traumatizing-generations-of-people/.

Blaufuss, Mary Schaller. "Unexpected Agents of God's Grace-ful Mission: Women's Participation in Christian Mass Movements in India." In *The God of All Grace: Essays in Honour of Origen Vasantha Jathanna*, edited by Joseph George, 441–51. Bangalore: Asian Trading Corporation and United Theological College, 2005.

Boehm, Sophie, and Clea Schumer. "10 Big Findings from the 2023 IPCC Report on Climate Change." World Resources Institute, March 20, 2023. https://www.wri.org/insights/2023-ipcc-ar6-synthesis-report-climate-change-findings/.

Breckenridge-Jackson, Ian. "Preserving History After Hurricane Katrina: In the Lower Ninth Ward, a Museum Works to Preserve a Culture Washed Away." *U.S. News and World Report*, August 25, 2015. https://www.usnews.com/news/articles/2015/08/25/preserving-history-after-hurricane-katrina/.

Brueggemann, Walter. *Genesis*. Interpretation: A Biblical Commentary for Teaching and Preaching. Louisville: Westminster John Knox, 1986.

Campbell-Nelson, John. "Bumi Tidak Tenang: Sebuah Studi Kasus tentang Gempa Bumi di Alor." In *Teologi Bencana: Pergumulan Iman dalam Konteks Bencana Alam dan Bencana Sosial*, edited by Zakaria Ngelow et al., 95–110. Makasar: Oase Intim, 2006.

———. "Religion and Disaster: A Critical Reflection Post Alor Earthquake 2004." In *Dealing with Diversity: Religion, Globalization, Violence, Gender and Disaster in Indonesia*, edited by Bernard Adeney-Risakotta, 317–34. Geneva: Globethics.net, 2014.

Carroll, S., and Theology of Disaster Resilience Working Group. "A Theology of Disaster Resilience in a Changing Climate (Framework Paper)." Sydney: Uniting World, 2019. https://www.churchagenciesnetwork.org.au/wp-content/uploads/2022/04/TDRCC-Framework.pdf.

Craddock, Fred. *Luke*. Interpretation: A Bible Commentary for Teaching and Preaching. Louisville: John Knox, 1990.

Diamond, Jared M. *Collapse: How Societies Choose to Fail or Succeed*. London: Penguin, 2005.

Elam, Stephanie. "A Flood Forced This Town to Move: It Could Be a Model for Others Hit by the Climate Crisis." *CNN*, July 17, 2019. https://www.cnn.com/2019/07/17/us/valmeyer-flooding-climate-crisis-midwest/index.html.

Emanuel, Kerry. *Divine Wind: The History and Science of Hurricanes*. London: Oxford University Press, 2005.

Environment and Society. "Paul Crutzen Popularizes the Concept of the Anthropocene." https://www.environmentandsociety.org/tools/keywords/paul-crutzen-popularizes-concept-anthropocene/.

Estrada, A. *La imposible teodicea*. Madrid: Trotta, 1997.

Farge, Emma, and Nidal Al-Mughrabi. "Gaza Death Toll: How Many Palestinians Has Israel's Offensive Killed?" *Reuters*, January 15, 2025. https://www.reuters.com/world/middle-east/how-many-palestinians-has-israels-gaza-offensive-killed-2025-01-15/.

Federal Emergency Management Agency (FEMA). "The Recovery Continuum." https://emilms.fema.gov/is_2900a/groups/28.html.

Fernandez, Eleazar S. "A Theology of Partnership in a Globalized World." *Review & Expositor* 113:1 (February 10, 2016) 23–31. https://journals.sagepub.com/doi/abs/10.1177/0034637315619004/.

Fiddes, Paul. "Creation Out of Love." In *The Work of Love: Creation as Kenosis*, edited by John Polkinghorne, 167–91. Grand Rapids: Eerdmans, 2001.

Freire, Paulo. *Pedagogy of the Oppressed*. 30th anniversary ed. New York and London: Continuum, 2000.

Fretheim, Terence E. *Creation Untamed: The Bible, God, and Natural Disasters*. Grand Rapids: Baker Academic, 2010.

———. "Divine Judgement and the Warming of the World: An Old Testament Perspective." In *God, Evil, and Suffering: Essays in Honor of Paul R. Sponheim*, edited by T. Fretheim and C. Thompson, 21–32. St. Paul, MN: Luther Seminary, 2000.

———. "The Plagues as Ecological Signs of Historical Disaster." *Journal of Biblical Literature* 110 (1991) 385–96.

———. *The Suffering of God: An Old Testament Perspective*. Overtures to Biblical Theology. Philadelphia: Fortress, 1984.

Bibliography

Global Ministries (Christian Church Disciples of Christ / United Church of Christ). Webinar "Disasters in Central America." March 5, 2021. https://www.globalministries.org/living-by-faith-overcoming-hurricanes-in-nicaragua-and-honduras/.

Gopp, Amy, and Brandon Gilvin, eds. *Help and Hope: Disaster Preparedness and Response Tools for Congregations*. Danvers, MA: Chalice, 2014.

Gutiérrez, Gustavo. *A Theology of Liberation: History, Politics, and Salvation*. Translated by Sister Caridad Inda and John Eagleson. Maryknoll, NY: Orbis, 1973.

Hart, David Bentley. *The Doors of the Sea*. Grand Rapids: Eerdmans, 2005.

Hawaii Department of Business, Economic Development and Tourism. "Maui Wildfire Impacts Economic Recovery." September 6, 2023. https://dbedt.hawaii.gov/blog/23-47/.

Hellman, Rachel. "A City Upon a Hill." *Belt Magazine*, May 14, 2021. https://beltmag.com/valmeyer-illinois-city-hill-mississippi-flood/.

Hefner, P. J. *The Human Factor*. Minneapolis: Fortress, 1993.

Hick, John. *Evil and the God of Love*. New York: Harper Collins, 1978.

Hokusai, Katsushika. *The Great Wave off Kanagawa*. 1830. Ukiyo-e (Woodblock print). Metropolitan Museum of Art, New York.

Howe, Janice V. *Nothing Ever Happens Here: A Guide to Disaster Ministry*. Exeter, NH: Publishing Works, 2008.

Huff, Barry R. "From Societal Scorn to Divine Delight: Job's Transformative Portrayal of Wild Animals." *Interpretation* 73:3 (2019) 248–58.

Integrated Research on Disaster Risk. *Peril Classification and Hazard Glossary*. March 2014. https://www.irdrinternational.org/upload/20240702/afc29fde2d2bb1.pdf.

Intergovernmental Panel on Climate Change. *Climate Change 2023: Synthesis Report; Summary for Policymakers*. https://www.ipcc.ch/report/ar6/syr/downloads/report/IPCC_AR6_SYR_SPM.pdf.

Katz, Jonathan M. *The Big Truck That Went By: How the World Came to Save Haiti and Left Behind a Disaster*. New York: St. Martin's Griffin, 2014.

Keller, Catherine. *Facing Apocalypse: Climate, Democracy, and Other Last Chances*. Maryknoll, NY: Orbis, 2021.

Klein, Naomi. *The Battle for Paradise: Puerto Rico Takes on the Disaster Capitalists*. Chicago: Haymarket, 2018.

———. *The Shock Doctrine: The Rise of Disaster Capitalism*. New York: Picador, 2008.

Klinenberg, Eric. *Palaces for the People: How Social Infrastructure Can Help Fight Inequality, Polarization, and the Decline of Civic Life*. New York: Crown, 2019.

Kolbert, Elizabeth. *Field Notes from a Catastrophe: Man, Nature, and Climate Change*. New York: Bloomsbury, 2015.

———. *The Sixth Extinction: An Unnatural History*. New York: Holt, 2014.

Kushner, Harold S. *When Bad Things Happen to Good People*. New York: Avon, 1981.

Lemos, Gregory, et al. "Tennessee Flooding Leaves 21 People Dead and Around 20 Others Missing." *CNN*, August 22, 2021. https://www.cnn.com/2021/08/22/us/tennessee-flooding/index.html.

Levin, Kelly, et al. "5 Big Findings from the IPCC's 2021 Climate Report." World Resources Institute, August 9, 2021. https://www.wri.org/insights/ipcc-climate-report/.

Lustgarten, Abrahm. "The Great Climate Migration." *New York Times*, July 23, 2023. https://www.nytimes.com/interactive/2020/07/23/magazine/climate-migration.html.

Mach, Katharine J., et al. "Managed Retreat Through Voluntary Buy-Outs of Flood Prone Properties." *Science Advances* 5:10 (October 9, 2019). https://www.science.org/doi/10.1126/sciadv.aax8995/.

Manchala, Deenabandhu. "Together in Hope Amidst the Pandemic: Exploring Partnership, Mission, and Public Theology." Schmiechen Public Lecture on Ministry. Eden Theological Seminary, St. Louis, October 30, 2020. https://youtu.be/oRfScu4oDqo?feature=shared&t=3596.

Matsa, Myrna. "Jewish Theology of Disaster and Recovery." DMin thesis, Hebrew Union College-Jewish Institute of Religion and Postgraduate Center for Mental Health, Los Angeles, 2006.

Mayer, B. "A Review of the Literature on Community Resilience and Disaster Recovery." *Current Environmental Health Report* 6 (2019) 167–73.

McCann, J. Clinton. "The Book of Job: Suffering, Creation, and Transformation." LIFE Certificate Course, September 2022, Eden Theological Seminary, St. Louis.

McKibben, Bill. *The Comforting Whirlwind: God, Job, and the Scale of Creation*. Grand Rapids: Eerdmans, 1994.

———. *Eaarth: Making a Life on a Tough New Planet*. New York: St. Martin's Griffin, 2010.

———. "Global Warming's Terrifying New Math." *Rolling Stone*, July 19, 2012. https://www.rollingstone.com/politics/politics-news/global-warmings-terrifying-new-math-188550/.

Midgett-Crosby, Brande. "Creation Justice Webinar on Climate Change and Forced Migration." United Church of Christ, February 19, 2019. http://www.ucc.org/creation_justice_webinar_on_climate_change_and_forced_migration/.

Moltmann, Jürgen. *The Crucified God: The Cross of Christ as the Foundation and Criticism of Christian Theology*. Translated by R. A. Wilson and J. Bowden. London: SCM, 1974.

———. "God's Kenosis in the Creation and Consummation of the World." In *The Work of Love: Creation as Kenosis*, edited by John Polkinghorne, 137–51. Grand Rapids: Eerdmans, 2001.

———. *Theology of Hope: On the Ground and Implications of a Christian Eschatology*. London: SCM, 1967.

Mwendo, Nilima, and Allison Plyer. "Beyond Data: Straight Talk from some Lower Ninth Ward Residents." Greater New Orleans Community Data

Center, Fall 2003. https://www.datacenterresearch.org/pre-katrina/orleans/8/22/cem/poverty.html.

National Interagency Coordination Center. "Wildland Fire Summary and Statistics Annual Report 2021." https://www.nifc.gov/sites/default/files/NICC/2-Predictive%20Services/Intelligence/Annual%20Reports/2021/annual_report_0.pdf.

National Voluntary Organizations Active in Disaster (NVOAD). *Light Our Way: A Guide for Spiritual Care in Times of Disaster for Disaster Response Volunteer, First Responders, and Disaster Planners*. 2018. https://www.nvoad.org/wp-content/uploads/light_our_way_2018_final-published-copy.pdf.

Patel, Sonny S., et al. "What Do We Mean by 'Community Resilience'? A Systematic Literature Review of How It Is Defined in the Literature." *PLoS Current* (February 1, 2017). https://www.ncbi.nlm.nih.gov/pmc/articles/PMC5693357/.

PBS News Hour. "Mississippi Approves Onshore Gambling as Biloxi Looks to Rebuild." *PBS News*, October 17, 2005. https://www.pbs.org/newshour/world/weather-july-dec05-rebuilding_biloxi/.

Peacocke, Arthur. "The Cost of New Life." In *The Work of Love: Creation as Kenosis*, edited by John Polkinghorne, 21–42. Grand Rapids: Eerdmans, 2001.

Polkinghorne, John. "Kenotic Creation and Divine Action." In *The Work of Love: Creation as Kenosis*, edited by John Polkinghorne, 90–106. Grand Rapids: Eerdmans, 2001.

Presbyterian Church (USA). *Book of Common Worship*. Louisville: Westminster John Knox, 2018.

Rafferty, John. "Superstorm Sandy." *Encyclopedia Britannica*, December 22, 2024. https://www.britannica.com/event/Superstorm-Sandy/.

Rumahuru, Yance Zadrak, and Augusthina Ch. Kakiay. "Rethinking Disaster Theology: Combining Protestant Theology with Local Knowledge and Modern Science in Disaster Response." In *Open Theology* (2020) 6:623–35. https://www.degruyter.com/document/doi/10.1515/opth-2020-0136/html?lang=en/.

Rich, Nathaniel. "Jungleland: The Lower Ninth Ward in New Orleans Gives New Meaning to 'Urban Growth.'" *New York Times*, March 21, 2012.

Rieger, Joerg. "Theology and Mission Between Colonialism and Postcolonialism." *Mission Studies* 21 (2004) 201–27.

Rolston, Holmes, III. "Kenosis and Nature." In *The Work of Love: Creation as Kenosis*, edited by John Polkinghorne, 43–65. Grand Rapids: Eerdmans, 2001.

Rossi, Marcello. "The Illinois Town That Got Up and Left." *BBC News*, March 14, 2022. https://www.bbc.com/future/article/20220310-the-illinois-town-valmeyer-could-be-a-model-for-relocation/.

BIBLIOGRAPHY

Santos, Rick. "What Led Me to This Moment—Reflections from CWS's New President and CEO." Church World Service (CWS), January 19, 2021. https://cwsglobal.org/blog/what-led-me-to-this-moment/.

Selig, Katie. "Youths Sued Montana Over Climate Change and Won. Why It Matters." *Washington Post*, August 16, 2023. https://www.washingtonpost.com/climate-environment/2023/08/17/montana-climate-lawsuit-impact/.

Shukman, David. "Climate Change: Summers Could Become 'Too Hot for Humans.'" *BBC News*, July 16, 2020. https://www.bbc.com/news/science-environment-53415298/.

Sobrino, Jon. *Christology at the Crossroads: A Latin American Approach.* Maryknoll, NY: Orbis, 1978.

———. *Christ the Liberator: A View from the Victims.* Maryknoll, NY: Orbis, 1999.

———. *Crucified Peoples.* Third World Theology. Translated by D. Livingstone. London: Catholic Institute for International Relations, 1990.

———. *Jesus the Liberator: A Historical-Critical Reading of Jesus of Nazareth.* Maryknoll, NY: Orbis, 1991.

———. *No Salvation Outside the Poor: Prophetic-Utopian Essays.* Maryknoll, NY: Orbis, 2008.

———. *The Principle of Mercy: Taking the Crucified People from the Cross.* Maryknoll, NY: Orbis, 1994.

———. *Spirituality of Liberation: Toward Political Holiness.* Maryknoll, NY: Orbis, 1990.

———. *The True Church and the Poor.* Repr. Eugene, OR: Wipf & Stock, 2004.

———. *Where Is God? Earthquake, Terrorism, Barbarity, and Hope.* Translated by Margaret Wilde. Maryknoll, NY: Orbis, 2006.

Southeast Florida Regional Climate Change Compact's Sea Level Rise Ad Hoc Work Group. "Unified Sea Level Rise Projection, Southeast Florida; 2019 Update." https://southeastfloridaclimatecompact.org/wp-content/uploads/2020/04/Sea-Level-Rise-Projection-Guidance-Report_FINAL_02212020.pdf.

Spivak, Gayatri Chakravorty. *A Critique of Postcolonial Reason: Toward a History of the Vanishing Present.* Cambridge: Harvard University Press, 1999.

St. Mary Catholic Church of the Seven Dolors of the Blessed Virgin. "History." https://stmaryvalmeyer.org/history.htm/.

Stanish, Stanley. "Reflecting Theologically on the Faith Responses of Tsunami Survivors." BD thesis, Tamil Nadu Theological Seminary, 2006.

Stern, Gary. *Can God Intervene? How Religion Explains Natural Disasters.* Westport, CT: Praeger, 2007.

Stevenson, Bryan. *Just Mercy: A Story of Justice and Redemption.* New York: Spiegel & Grau, 2014.

Swain, Storm. *Trauma and Transformation at Ground Zero: A Pastoral Theology.* Minneapolis: Fortress, 2011.

BIBLIOGRAPHY

Talukdar, Foezullah. "Implications of the Combination of Climate-Change and COVID-19 Induced Poverty." Eden Theology Seminary, St. Louis, October 8, 2020. https://www.youtube.com/watch?v=_3zrVQHdOeM.

Tharakan, Parayil A. "A Tsunami Story." *Song of the Waves* (blog), March 22, 2011. http://parayilat.blogspot.com/2011/03/tsunami-story.html.

Tinker, George. "An American Indian Theological Response to Ecojustice." In *Defending Mother Earth: Native American Perspective on Environmental Justice*, edited by Jace Weaver, 153–76. Maryknoll, NY: Orbis, 1996.

Tino, Caterina. "WCC's Engagement for Children." World Council of Churches, November 21, 2018. https://www.youtube.com/watch?v=Pyt4a5u7JZg&index=5&list=PLI22eVXX9FYmSQkUcA69sIGeJEcwyxGeg/.

Turner, Victor. *The Ritual Process: Structure and Anti-Structure*. Foundations of Human Behavior. London and New York: Routledge, 2017.

Uili, A. S., et al. "A Theology of Disaster Resilience in a Changing Climate, Bible Studies." Sydney: Uniting World, 2019. https://anglicanoverseasaid.org.au/wp-content/uploads/2023/08/Theology-of-Disaster-Resilience-Bible-Studies.pdf.

United Church of Christ. "Justice for #EachGeneration." http://www.eachgeneration.org/.

United Nations International Strategy for Disaster Reduction (UNISDR). "Terminology: Basic Terms of Disaster Risk Reduction." March 31, 2004. https://www.unisdr.org/files/7817_7819isdrterminology11.pdf.

United Nations Office for Disaster Risk Reduction (UNDRR). "Resilience." https://www.undrr.org/terminology/resilience/.

United States Geological Survey (USGS). "How Can Climate Change Affect Natural Disasters?" https://www.usgs.gov/faqs/how-can-climate-change-affect-natural-disasters/.

Wallace-Wells, David. "2019–2020 Australian Bushfires." Center for Disaster Philanthropy, December 31, 2019. https://disasterphilanthropy.org/disasters/2019-australian-wildfires/.

———. "Global Apathy Toward the Fires in Australia Is a Scary Portent for the Future." *New York Magazine*, December 31, 2019. https://nymag.com/intelligencer/2019/12/new-south-wales-fires-in-australia-the-worlds-response.html.

Weber, Anna, and Rob Moor. "Going Under: Long Wait Times for Post-Flood Buyouts Leave Homeowners Under Water." Natural Resources Defense Council, September 2019. https://www.nrdc.org/sites/default/files/going-under-post-flood-buyouts-report.pdf.

Wesley, John. "Serious Thoughts Occasioned by the Late Earthquake in Lisbon." In *The Works of John Wesley*. 14 vols. 3rd ed. Edited by Thomas Jackson. Repr. Grand Rapids: Baker, 1979.

White, Robert S. *Who Is to Blame? Disasters, Nature, and Acts of God*. Oxford and Grand Rapids: Monarch, 2014.

Williams, Rowan. "Of Course This Makes Us Doubt God's Existence." *Telegraph* (London) January 2, 2005.

Bibliography

World Council of Churches and ACT Alliance. *Called to Transformation: Ecumenical Diakonia*. Geneva: World Council of Churches Publications, 2022.

Location Index

United States

Arizona, Grand Canyon, 54, 56
Florida, 13, 26, 84
Hawaii 28, 54
Illinois, Valmeyer, 132–34
Louisiana, New Orleans, 7, 65, 82–86, 91–93, 118, 126–27, 129, 135–36
Mississippi River, 58
Mississippi, Biloxi, 7, 63–64, 82, 94–97, 111–12
Missouri, Ferguson, 14
Missouri, Hermann, 80–81
Montana, Glacier National Park, 121–24
New York, Love Canal, 13
New York, New York City, 13, 147–48
New York, Watkins Glen, 54
North Dakota, 84, 90
Oklahoma, Moore, 65
South Carolina, 90
Tennessee, 10, 129
Texas, Houston, 129
Texas, Jefferson County (Beaumont and Port Arthur), 118–19

Global

Afghanistan, 10, 110
Australia, 27–28
Bangladesh, 13, 17, 127–28
Burundi, 11, 149
Democratic Republic of the Congo, 149
Egypt, 41
El Salvador, 103–8, 125–26, 149
Ethiopia, 11, 149
Guatemala, 149
Haiti, 9–10, 54, 65–66, 77, 100–102
Honduras, 149
India, Kerala, 24
Indonesia, 90, 128, 130
Japan, 13, 131
Kenya, 11, 149
Malawi, 11, 149
Nepal, 113–14

Location Index

Pakistan, 11
Palestine–Gaza, 11–12
Philippines, 98, 117–18
Portugal, Lisbon, 21–23
Puerto Rico, 89, 99, 149

Rwanda, 11, 149

Sri Lanka, 137–38

Sudan, 11, 149
Syria, 149

Tanzania, 11, 149
Tuvalu, 13, 17, 153–56

Uganda, 11, 149
Ukraine, 11

Vietnam (Mekong Delta), 149

Named Disaster Events Index

Earthquake 2010, Haiti, 9, 54, 65–66, 77, 100–102

Earthquake 2015, Nepal, 113–14

Earthquake 2001, El Salvador, 103–8

Hurricane Betsy 1965, Louisiana, 92

Hurricane Fifi 1974, Honduras, Guatemala, El Salvador, 103

Hurricane Harvey 2017, Texas, 26

Hurricane Irene 2011, Caribbean and East Coast United States, 26, 149

Hurricane Katrina 2005, Florida, Louisiana, Mississippi, 7–8, 63–64, 82–86, 91–93, 94–97, 111–12, 118, 126–27, 129, 135–36

Hurricane Maria 2017, Puerto Rico, 26, 89, 99

Hurricane Mitch 1999, Honduras, Guatemala, El Salvador, 103

Superstorm Sandy 2012, Caribbean and Mid-Atlantic United States, 26

Tsunami and Earthquake 2004, India, Indonesia, Somalia, Sri Lanka, Thailand, 3–5, 23–24, 90, 128, 130, 137–38

Typhoon Haiyan 2013, Philippines, 98, 117–18

Wildfires (Bushfires) 2019–2020, Australia, 25–28

Scripture Index

Genesis

1	47, 50
2: 1–3	71
2: 22–33	71
3: 16–19	53
6–9	53, 75
6: 11–13	75
8: 1	53
45: 3–11, 15	150–52

2 Kings

2	76

Job

38, 46–47, 49–51, 59, 61, 71, 75, 155

Psalms

8	50
37	38
73	38
104: 30	50, 58, 155

Isaiah

11: 1–9	73, 79
35: 1–10	73, 79
65: 17–25	73, 79

Jeremiah

4: 22–26	75
29: 7	138

Micah

4:3	130

Matthew

10:16	110
23: 11–12	139
28: 18–20	141–43

Luke

4: 1–13	88
13: 1–9	37–38

John

9:2	38, 47–48
10:10	93

Acts

1	143

1 Corinthians

12: 26	39

Scripture Index

Ephesians

1:10   139

Author/People Index

Antal, Jim, 27

Bhagwan, James, 153–54
Bonds, Dale and Jim, 135–36
Bracke, John, 36
Brueggemann, Walter, 36, 150–51

Campbell-Nelson, John, 130
Carroll, Seforosa, 155–56
Caterina (El Salvador), 104–5
Che, Ines (El Salvador), 104
Craddock, Fred, 39
Coppola, Florence, 83
Crutzen, Paul, 17

Davy, Charles, 22

Fernandez, Eleazar, 136
Fiddes, Paul, 74
Fonderlin, Diane, 137–38
Friere, Paulo, 41
Fretheim, Terence, 36–37, 49–53, 56–58, 69–71, 73–75, 78–80

Gerholdt, Rhys, 27
Gutiérrez, Gustavo, 41

Hart, David Bentley, 24
Hefner, P. J., 72
Heidegger, Martin, 42
Hokusai, Katsushika, 131–32
Howe, Janice, 116
Howe, Katie, 116
Huff, Barry, 49

Katz, Jonathan, 100

Kakjay, Augusthina Ch., 129
Kant, Immanuel, 2
Keller, Catherine, 16, 50, 60, 70–72
Klein, Naomi, 99
Klinenberg, Eric, 26, 136
Knobloch, Dennis, 133–34
Kolbert, Elizabeth, 17–18, 52
Kushner, Harold, 68

Lustgarten, Abrahm, 149–50

Makewin, Koloma, 155–56
Manchala, Deenabandhu, 128, 138–39
Matsa, Myrna, 51, 91
Maier, Harry O., 60
Malcolm, Michael, 151
McCann, J. Clinton, 50
McKibben, Bill, 16, 50, 60
Moltmann, Jürgen, 69–70, 73

Oommen, Kiran, 152–53

Peacocke, Arthur, 55–57
Pinter, Nicholas, 133
Polkinghorne, John, 54, 70, 72
Prestemon, Shari, 96–97

Rich, Nathaniel, 91
Rieger, Joerg, 137
Rolston, Holmes, 70
Rumahuru, Yance Zadrak, 128–29

Sanders, Susan, 83

Author/People Index

Sobrino, Jon, 41, 103–8, 120, 125
Spivak Gayatri, 34
Stern, Gary, 24
Stevenson, Bryan, 87
Swain, Storm, 147–48

Talukdar, Foezullah, 128
Thompson, Karen Georgia, 84
Tinker, George, 136
Tino, Caterina, 152–53

Turner, Victor, 32
Tutu, Desmond, 136

Voltaire, 23

Wallace-Wells, David, 27
Waskow, David, 27
Weiss, Harvey, 17
White, Robert S., 35
Williams, Rowan, 24
Wolgemuth, Zach, 98–99, 117–19

Subject and Organization Index

A Christian Ministry in the National Parks, 121
Accompaniment, 84–86, 88, 117–20, 124
Accountability, 15, 29, 30–34, 35, 66, 69, 75–80, 83, 88, 113, 117–19, 142–43, 145
ACT Alliance, 113
Act of God, 15, 23, 45, 142
Adaptation, 12, 16–17, 134, 146, 150–51, 153, 156
Advocacy, 27, 60, 85, 87, 98, 150, 156
Authenticity, 15, 19, 30–36, 46, 69, 72–74, 77–79, 88, 90, 119, 142–43
Authority, 15, 30, 32–34, 67, 77, 88, 110, 119, 132, 142–43

Behemoth, 52
Back Bay Mission, 7, 63–64, 82, 94–97, 111–12

Calvinism, 29–30
Cancer, 1–3, 59
Chaos, 4, 19, 32, 35, 49–56, 60–61, 66, 80–81, 136, 143
Capacity, 89, 113, 117–18, 137
Christian Commission for Development in Bangladesh, 128
Church World Service, 114
Clean Slate, 6, 94, 98–99, 118, 139

Climate Change, 10–13, 16–19, 26–27, 32–34, 46, 52, 59–61, 77, 107, 112–14, 118, 128, 144, 149–56
Climate Refugees, 9, 12, 149
Co-Creators, 71–74, 77
Community Organizations Active in Disaster, 112
Community Organizing, 150
Complex Creation, 49, 55–56, 60, 69, 72, 76–78, 87, 138, 140
Complex Order, 33, 42–43, 45–46, 49, 52–54, 56, 58, 60–61, 68, 70, 73, 77, 138, 140–42
Conference of the Parties (COP), 114
Continuing Creation, 18, 49, 57–59, 61, 68–69, 74–75, 77–79, 111, 127–28, 154
Coronavirus, 11, 15, 36
Covenant of Compassion, 82–83
Creation Theology, 43–61, 70
Crucified Peoples, 103–8

Disaster Capitalism, 6
Disaster Risk Reduction, 145–46
Discipleship, 155–56
Doing Theology, 32–37

Eaarth, 60
Enlightenment, 21, 23, 48, 52, 67
Equity, 16, 30, 111, 118–19

Subject and Organization Index

FEMA, 13, 89, 101, 112–13, 115–16, 129, 133–34
Fractals, 55
Fuller Disaster Rebuilders, 100
Global Ministries (Christian Church Disciples of Christ / United Church of Christ), 107, 117, 128, 130, 137–38
Good Not Perfect, 56–57, 70–71
Grace-ful Mission, 125
The Great Wave Off Kanagawa, 131–32

Hermeneutic Circle, 41
Huracán, 51

IMA World Health, 109–10
Innovative, 132–36
Intergovernmental Panel on Climate Change, 10–11, 16, 27
Just Rebuilding, 83, 91, 93–94, 109, 111, 117
Justice, 30, 85, 88, 93, 98, 107, 109–20, 125, 128, 144, 152–55

Kadamma, 51
Kenosis, 69–71, 75
Kamikaze, 130–31
Kodalamma, 24

Leviathan, 52
Liberation, 103
Light Our Way, 147
Liminality, 19, 32–34
Liturgical, 20, 25, 42, 80
Long Term, 2–3, 8–10, 13–19, 40, 56, 83–85, 87–90, 101, 111–18, 126, 141–56

National Voluntary Organizations Active in Disaster (NVOAD), 112, 115, 119, 147
New Normal, 40, 125–26, 128, 139

Open-Ended, 45–46, 49, 56–58, 61, 68

Our Children's Trust, 153
Pacific Conference of Churches, 153–56
Partnership, 83, 101, 112, 114, 119, 136, 137–38, 140
Period Doubling, 55
Pluralism, 52
Postmodernity, 52
Praxic Theodicy, 107–8, 119–20
Prolonged Disaster, 148–49
Puertopia, 99
Proximity, 86

Quantum Worldview, 52

Randomness, 4, 38, 40, 43, 45, 49, 55, 60–61, 63–68, 87, 125, 130, 137–39
Redemption, 12, 18, 59, 79, 111, 140
Resilient community, 15, 18–19, 73, 125, 141, 121–40, 144, 145–50, 152, 155

Southeast Texas Community Development Corporation, 119
Situational, 130–32
Solidarity, 84–85, 88, 90, 107–8, 109–20, 125, 128, 154–56
State Voluntary Organizations Active in Disaster, 112
Subaltern Studies Collective, 34
Sustainable Community, 1, 18
Sustaining Love, 126–28, 141–56

Theodicy, 66–68, 78
Theotopia, 71

Ubuntu, 39
United Church of Christ, 8, 27, 63, 82–84, 89, 100, 109, 116–17, 119, 126, 138, 149, 151–52
United Church of Christ in the Philippines, 98–99, 117–18
United Nations Children's Fund (UNICEF), 152–53

Subject and Organization Index

United Nations Framework Convention on Climate Change, 114

United Nations International Strategy for Disaster Reduction, 14

United Nations Office of Disaster Risk Reduction, 145

Uniting Church in Australia, 155

World Council of Churches, 152–53

World Health Organization (WHO), 36

www.ingramcontent.com/pod-product-compliance
Lightning Source LLC
Chambersburg PA
CBHW020850160426
43192CB00007B/855